W9-ALL-189

RESTORING
THE STATUE OF
LIBERTY

RESTORING
THE STATUE OF
LIBERTY

SCULPTURE · STRUCTURE · SYMBOL

RICHARD SETH HAYDEN · THIERRY W. DESPONT

with
NADINE M. POST

photographs by DAN CORNISH

McGRAW-HILL BOOK COMPANY

New York   St. Louis   San Francisco   Auckland   Bogotá   Hamburg
Johannesburg   London   Madrid   Mexico   Montreal   New Delhi
Panama   Paris   São Paulo   Singapore   Sydney   Tokyo   Toronto

974.7g
Hay

Library of Congress Cataloging-in-Publication Data
Hayden, Richard Seth.
  Restoring the Statue of Liberty.

  Includes bibliographies and index.
  1. Statue of Liberty (New York, N.Y.) 2. Statue of
Liberty National Monument (New York, N.Y.) 3. New York
(N.Y.)—Buildings, structures, etc. I. Despont,
Thierry W. II. Post, Nadine M. III. Title.
F128.64.L6H38 1986   974.7′1   85-30133
ISBN 0-07-027327-8
ISBN 0-07-027326-X (pbk.)
ISBN 0-07-027328-6 (deluxe)

Photographs © 1986 by Dan Cornish, unless otherwise indicated.
The historical photographs are courtesy of the U.S. Department of
the Interior, National Park Service.

1234567890   KGP/KGP   8932109876

ISBN 0-07-027327-8

ISBN 0-07-027326-X {PBK.}

ISBN 0-07-027328-6 {DELUXE}

Sponsoring Editor: Joan Zseleczky
Editing Supervisor: Jim Bessent
Design Supervisor: Mark E. Safran
Production Supervisor: Teresa F. Leaden

The typesetting and the color separation for this book were done by
York Graphic Services, Inc. The typeface is ITC Berkeley Oldstyle
Medium.

Printed and bound by The Kingsport Press.

This book is dedicated to the women in our lives:
Eleanor and Francette,
Pamela and Ann,
Melanie and Hillary, Catherine and Louise,
and the Statue

CONTENTS

Centennial Year of Liberty in the United States

By the President of the United States of America

A Proclamation

She remains a Wonder of the World—an uncanny fusion of art and engineering. She is the result of a unique collaboration between two freedom-loving Frenchmen with a profound affection for America: a great sculptor, Frederic-Auguste Bartholdi, and the greatest structural engineer of his time, Alexandre Gustave Eiffel. Next year she will be 100 years old.

Nineteen hundred and eighty-six marks the Centennial of the Statue of Liberty. Originally called "Liberty Enlightening the World," the Statue was a generous gift from the people of France to the people of the United States. It represents the close and cordial relationship that traditionally has existed between our countries and our common devotion to freedom and democracy.

She rises majestically 151 feet above the magnificent base designed by Richard M. Hunt, the preeminent American architect. But she is much more than her awesome dimensions and her physical splendor. For millions of anxious immigrants, the forebears of countless millions of today's Americans, she was the first glimpse of America. She was assurance of journey's end, safe harbor reached at last, and the beginning of a new adventure in a free and blessed land. For them she was a dream come true, the Lady with the Lamp, a warm welcome to a new world and a new life.

The gifted American poet Emma Lazarus, hailing her as the "New Colossus," put the message of the Statue of Liberty in unforgettable words:

> Keep ancient lands, your storied pomp . . .
> Give me your tired, your poor,
> Your huddled masses yearning to breathe free,
> The wretched refuse of your teeming shore.
> Send these, the homeless, tempest-tost, to me.
> I lift my lamp beside the Golden Door.

Since its dedication on October 28, 1886, the Statue of Liberty has held high the beacon of freedom, hope, and opportunity to welcome millions of immigrants and visitors from foreign lands. From that time she has been one of the proudest symbols of the American ideal of liberty and justice for all.

Today, the Statue of Liberty and nearby Ellis Island are being restored from the ravages of time and weather by the Statue of Liberty-Ellis Island Centennial Foundation, Inc.

The United States will celebrate the one hundredth anniversary of the Statue of Liberty through commemorative events scheduled to take place during the Fourth of July Weekend in 1986 and on October 28, 1986.

In recognition of the importance of the Statue of Liberty to the American people, the Congress, by House Joint Resolution 407, has designated the twelve-month period ending on October 28, 1986, as the "Centennial Year of Liberty in the United States" and authorized and requested the President to issue a proclamation in observance of this occasion.

NOW, THEREFORE, I, RONALD REAGAN, President of the United States of America, do hereby proclaim the twelve-month period ending on October 28, 1986, as the Centennial Year of Liberty in the United States, and I call upon the people of the United States to observe this year with appropriate ceremonies and activities.

IN WITNESS WHEREOF, I have hereunto set my hand this twenty-eighth day of October, in the year of our Lord nineteen hundred and eighty-five, and of the Independence of the United States of America the two hundred and tenth.

Ronald Reagan

ACKNOWLEDGMENTS

The origins of this book lie somewhere between a boat ride to the Statue of Liberty and a walk in the gardens of Versailles. Somehow we knew that our task would not be complete without an account of the dedication and labor of the hundreds who worked with us to restore the statue. The restoration experience has been and will continue to be an invaluable one for ourselves and, we think, for all involved. We will treasure the friendships and the memories.

* * *

Of the members of the restoration team, Bob Landsman, Blaine Cliver, and John Robbins stand out for their extraordinary commitment to see the statue properly restored. Without them, her lamp would not shine as brightly beside the golden door. Ed Cohen and Howard Brandston, Dave Moffitt, Bob Cahill, Ross Holland, Larry Bellante, Gene McGovern, Phil Kleiner, and Jay Gang all contributed more than their share and should be seen as the true authors of this book.

In a project of this magnitude it is almost impossible to acknowledge everyone's contribution, but we must at least mention those who came to inspire or challenge us personally during the past five years. Therefore our special thanks:

To Albert Swanke, whose wise advice guided us throughout the project. To our French colleagues, Philippe Grandjean, Jean Levron, Jacques Moutard, and Pierre Tissier, who taught us again the joy and pain of an international collaboration.

To the Statue of Liberty–Ellis Island Foundation: Lee Iacocca, whose enlightened leadership made this project possible; and Paul Bergmoser, Bill May, Steve Breganti, Palmer Wald, Gary Kelly, Denver Frederick, Paula Victor, Henning Nielsen, Penny Becker, Budd Pettibone, and Robert Kraus.

To the foundation agonists: Paul Windels, Susan Snyder, and Roger D'Amecourt, whose commitment to the project made our participation possible.

To the Department of the Interior and the National Park Service: the Honorable Donald Hodel, Russell Dickenson, William Mott, Herbert Cables, Charles Clapper, Garnett Chapin, Diane Adams, Kevin

Buckley, and Bill Dehart. A special mention to Carole Perrault; Caroline Veille, her assistant in France; and consultant Norman Nielsen; whose diligent research contributed immensely to the historical and metallurgical documentation of the Statue's history.

To the Restoration Coordination Committee, Herb Barchoff, Nick Cretan, Bernard Eichwald, Capt. Jim McDonald (U.S.C.G), Steve Oster, Paul Preus, and Hans Schaefer.

To the Architectural Advisory Group, the Honorable George White, Jean–Paul Carlian, Robert Louis Geddes, Maurice Novarina, Charles Thornton, and Jeb Turner.

To our consultants, Angela Baltaian, Vito Cerami, Bill DiGiacomo, Pat DiNapoli, Paul Emilius, James Hauser, Marvin Kass, Colin Landrigan, Jordan Steckel, Gene Stival, John Van Deusen, and Joe Velozi.

Among the members of our offices, Joe Colt, Don Kiehl, and Bill Koelling for their unselfish contributions throughout the project.

To the design team in our offices, Gae Buckley, Juan Bustamante, Lucien Coste, Michael Cullinen, David Duchai, Jeremiah King, Peter McGinley, Robin Moore, David Pitches, Dom Scali, Laura Schwartz, Ronald Skrobe, Michael Watson, and Jay Walter.

To the foundation staff architects and engineers, George Evans and Craig Smith.

To the construction manager, Lehrer/McGovern: Peter Lehrer, Peter Gould, John Fontana, Jim Genovese, Sandy Ginsberg, George Hoehl, Mark Ospala, Tom Peters, and Raymond Totillo; and on the site, Manoocher Akhtarshenas, Angelo J. Anello, Frank Briguglio, Shawn Doran, and Harold Lyons.

Our special thanks to those whose support and guidance helped us in many ways: Ed Connell and Richard Carlson, Peter Herman, Jean Pierre Bardon, and Mayor Edmond Gerrer and Pierre Burger in Colmar, and Barry LePatner, who at times seemed to be a full member of the team.

We owe a special debt of gratitude to those at McGraw-Hill—Joan Zseleczky, our tireless editor; Hal Crawford; Eileen Kramer; Terry Leaden; Jim Bessent; Mark Safran; and Steve Boldish—and in our own offices—Mary-Jo Burke, Howard Katz, Don Lunetta, and Karen Small—whose efforts helped make this book a reality.

Our sincere thanks to Jimmy Salazar and Jaime Storms at 400 Park Avenue for their cheers at our late hours exits, and to Giuseppe, who could always make us laugh.

To Patricia McGonigle for her perpetual good humor and tireless efforts and to Lindsey Hall for her steady and unceasing assistance, our sincere gratitude.

Our warmest appreciation to Nadine Post and Dan Cornish, whose creative talents contributed greatly to this book.

To Bartholdi, Eiffel, and Hunt, our confraternal salutations.

To our fathers, Joseph and Guy, our hats.

PREFACE

On July 4, 1984, the flame of the Statue of Liberty was brought down for restoration amid a crowd of cheerful onlookers. As the flame was slowly lowered along the giant scaffold that surrounded the statue, conversation and cheers became muted and the mood of the crowd turned pensive. Since the statue's inauguration on October 28, 1886, the flame had grown to symbolize liberty, and at that moment all present seemed to realize how fragile liberty is and how much care is needed to maintain it.

Among those present, the authors were especially moved. For them, the lowering of the flame was not only the official beginning of the centennial restoration but the culmination of more than two years of research and planning. They knew that over the next two years the contributions and efforts of thousands would be needed before the crowd could gather again for the glorious celebration of the statue's rededication.

This book is a companion piece to the centennial restoration, an account left for future generations by the architects who assembled and led the design team. It is a thank-you to the millions who gave money, the thousands the project touched, and the hundreds with whom they worked.

Here is a fascinating story that began more than 100 years ago in France to reach a climax in America on July 4, 1986, the statue's centennial. Like her beginnings, the restoration of the Statue of Liberty is a tale of challenge and dedication: the tale of how a colossal sculpture, the tallest structure of its time, became America's most cherished symbol; how a gift of such magnitude was conceived of and offered by a group of French people; how 100 years later, supported by the generosity of the people of the United States, a team of architects and engineers, workers, artisans, and technicians came together to restore the statue.

This journal will draw you into her past and show you how decisions made by her creators and caretakers had a profound impact on the restorers' work. It will tell you of the uncanny parallels, the similarities, and the differences between the original construction and the restoration.

The Statue of Liberty.

As the flame was slowly lowered along the giant scaffold . . . July 4, 1984.

It explains how the restoration of the statue as a sculpture would call upon the resources of historians and fine-arts specialists, how the renovation of the structure would challenge architects and engineers, how traditional craftsmanship was blended with modern technology, how the demands of preservation, restoration, and renovation came together to give new life to the symbol.

The statue's spirit carried the team through it all and provided the inspiration to unravel her puzzles and restore her for 100 or even 1000 years. In the end, the final gift of the project was her gift to the team, not the team's to her.

Come on a journey through the statue's time and spaces. Roam around her scaffold high above New York harbor. Share the joys, the frustrations; the problems, the solutions; the mysteries, the discoveries.

Turn the pages and begin the journey. Be mesmerized by the statue's beauty, her quiet power and immortality.

Come join in our celebration of Liberty!

Dismantling the flame, July 3, 1984.

RESTORING
THE STATUE OF
LIBERTY

THE TEAM

In a century the centenary of independence will be cele-
brated again. We shall then be only forgotten dust. Amer-
ica, who will then have more than a hundred millions of
inhabitants, will be ignorant of our names. But the Statue
will remain.

EDOUARD DE LABOULAYE
Journalist
from his address to the
Franco-American Union 1875

The project for the restoration of the Statue of Liberty required an
army of experts and countless hours of research and design,
many in extraordinarily diverse settings. Discussion, debate, and decision making took place not only in offices and at the statue itself but
also on planes and in boats, in cabs and on street corners, in both
Europe and the United States. For over five years, the statue project
spilled outside the routine workday to touch the lives of those participating.

Our initial task, early in 1982, was to assemble the American design team to complement the French consultants who had focused
attention on the poor condition of the statue. This *groupement* of consultants—architect-engineer Philippe Grandjean, metal expert Jacques
Moutard, structural engineer Pierre Tissier, and mechanical engineer
Jean Levron—had already prepared a white paper identifying the statue's major problems. It was their research and diagnostic work that
gave the project much of its initial momentum.

Grandjean is a graduate of the Ecole Polytechnique and has a
diploma in architecture from the Ecole Nationale des Beaux-Arts, giv-
ing him engineering training combined with a traditional architectural
education. He is levelheaded and inquisitive. Throughout the early
phase of the project, he probed and formulated theories which provided important stimuli to the research even if they were impractical at
times.

Jacques Moutard is a *compagnon,* a master artisan who began
working in the family shop when he was twelve years old. His life had
been dedicated to ornamental metal crafts and especially to the
repoussé technique of forming metal. It was Moutard's curiosity about
the statue's condition that led to the *groupement's* involvement in the
centennial restoration.

Carrying the torch.

3

Origin of the idea: The seeds of the project were planted in 1865 at a dinner at Glatigny, the home of Bartholdi's friend and supporter, Edouard de Laboulaye, a writer-teacher-politician and authority on America. At that dinner, attended by Bartholdi, Laboulaye envisioned a monument that would celebrate Franco-American friendship and symbolize the American dream of liberty. It took ten years and a change of government in France for the project to become a reality. Then, Laboulaye and his friends formed the French-American Union to raise funds and build in France a statue in the form of La liberté éclairant le monde (Liberty Enlightening the World), *the world's most colossal sculpture. The statue was completed in Paris in 1884, sent to the United States, and dedicated on October 28, 1886.*

The team was fortunate to have Moutard and came to rely on his judgment relative to the nature of metalwork and the art of repoussé. Moreover, although he did not speak any English, his calm and patient demeanor was much appreciated when discussions became heated. Moutard was always a quiet participant, willing to listen endlessly to the more vocal members of the team before making a point that considered another person's argument. He also kept the team amply supplied with an excellent champagne from his native village, Le Ricet.

Tissier is a structural engineer experienced in designing and restoring light metal structures. He had worked with Grandjean on other projects as an independent consultant. Tissier proposed working with the Centre des Etudes Techniques des Industries Métallurgiques (CETIM), one of the foremost research centers on metal structures in France. CETIM engineers had just completed an analysis for the restoration of the Eiffel Tower. This was important because Alexandre-Gustave Eiffel had also engineered the structural framework of the statue. His tower, built soon after the statue, used similar materials.

Tissier was the most French of all the French consultants. Robust, with a full-bearded face reminiscent of Victor Hugo, Tissier was committed to saving the statue and, despite the language barrier, to "enlightening those friendly, if somewhat uncultured, Americans".

A mechanical engineer with a successful practice in Paris, Levron was the only one of the French consultants who had experience working outside France. He contributed his mechanical engineering expertise as well as his strong business sense. He gave coherence to the working organization of Grandjean, Tissier, and Moutard.

On the basis of the *groupement's* white paper, the National Park Service, the bureau within the U.S. Department of the Interior charged with the statue's care, had asked that a detailed diagnostic report be prepared to explore in depth the condition of the statue. This sparked the formation of the French-American Committee for the Restoration of the Statue of Liberty, created, like its counterpart the French-American Union more than 100 years ago, to raise funds from French and American citizens to pay for work on the statue. Both French and American business executives served on the committee.

The authors with Colmar Mayor Edmond Gerrer (right) and Robert Landsman (left).

Through her persistence, Susan Leland Snyder, the treasurer of the French-American Committee, enrolled support for the restoration long before it had become a popular cause. Paul Windels, a New York lawyer, accepted the American presidency of the committee.

As it was clear that the work was broader in scope than originally expected, the committee decided that the project needed strong American participation. The job was too complicated and distant for the French consultants alone. Most of the construction work would be done by American contractors, and the *groupement* was not familiar with American design standards, construction procedures, and customary business practice.

On behalf of the committee, Snyder approached Albert Homer Swanke of Swanke Hayden Connell Architects about the project. Swanke, with impressive professional accomplishments, and very much an elder statesman in architectural circles, has a sharp mind that can cut to the heart of any issue. The firm had experience in historic restoration, including such projects as the original Senate and Supreme Court chambers in the U.S. Capitol. Although Swanke himself was about to retire and was not willing to become involved professionally, the firm was interested in participating.

* * *

Richard Hayden: "As the firm's managing partner, I made the commitment to stay personally involved, spending the time necessary for a project of this historic importance. I enjoy the challenge of leading large and diverse teams required for complex projects such as the statue's restoration."

Thierry Despont: "At about the same time I was contacted by Levron on behalf of the committee. Having been educated in France and the United States, I knew American and French design and construction customs and had established an international firm based in New York City and dedicated to the practice of architecture in the Beaux-Arts tradition. I love classical architecture and welcomed the opportunity to become involved in the statue restoration. I went to

Paris to meet with Grandjean and his associates. They showed me the white paper for the Park Service. It was a solid piece of work that identified the main problems of the statue, although put together very quickly and leaving many questions unanswered."

The French-American Committee had, by the time of this Paris meeting, signed an agreement with the National Park Service for the diagnostic report and had formally asked Swanke Hayden Connell to participate as the American architect for the restoration project. The committee set out to raise money to pay for the study. It was the spring of 1982, and the wheels of the project were beginning to turn.

Thierry Despont: "Upon my return to New York, I contacted Hayden and we met to discuss our mutual interest in the project. At that point, Hayden asked my firm to join as associate architect for the project, thereby forming the core of the American design team."

*   *   *

A second engineering consultant was needed. The structural design and analysis required were complex, with many unknown elements. Peer review was necessary on all structural matters. As the statue's engineering is similar to that of a bridge, the project would benefit from an engineer with experience in bridge design.

In Paris, 1884.

The statue completed in Paris, 1884.

7

This led the team to Edward Cohen, chief executive officer of Ammann & Whitney, Inc., who was invited to join as structural consultant for the diagnostic phase. Cohen became a valuable team member. He is a brilliant engineer who has directed Ammann & Whitney for more than a decade. His firm had tackled such enormous projects as the Whitestone and Verrazano bridges in New York.

Cohen and Tissier quickly developed a fine working relationship. Likely as not, after Cohen had made a presentation, Tissier would disagree and declare, "Absolument pas." They would then argue the merits of their respective proposals and eventually come to a mutually agreeable solution. Cohen would then say, "I agree with Monsieur Tissier," and Tissier would say, "Of course you do."

The National Park Service indicated that it would provide strong support in the area of essential historical documentation. In concert with it, the design team decided to do its own research to unravel the statue's mysteries. A talented photographer with acrobatic skills was needed to record every detail of the project. Dan Cornish became an important member of the team.

In the winter of 1982–1983, the American team took turns with its French colleagues in traveling between Paris and New York to prepare the diagnostic report and complete the research on the project. This discovery phase was fascinating. The team began to learn of the brilliance of the original design and to define the scope of work required for the restoration.

Paris is the city of the statue's birth, and her presence there is still strong today. Replicas of the statue remain on the Seine and in the Jardin du Luxembourg. Throughout the city, the spirit that conceived, created, and promoted the statue can be felt.

Bartholdi's and Eiffel's many works in Paris were visited. The American team also went to Bartholdi's birthplace, Colmar, to see his museum, full of sketches, papers, study models, and other memorabilia. A point was made to see all his works—large or small, good or bad.

In France, tradition and modern technology coexist. Artisans continue the skills of past days, combining them with up-to-date methods

8

Philippe Grandjean, Edward Cohen, and Blaine Cliver in Paris. (Small Moon Enterprises.)

and materials. In some surviving shops, or ateliers, the repoussé technique of hammering copper, used to shape the statue's skin, is being performed in much the same way as it was 100 years ago, mostly for decorative restoration work. The team visited these shops to understand and appreciate how the statue was built.

At first, the project was organized so that the French consultants would be leading the diagnostic and design phases and the Americans would assume responsibility for implementation. This soon proved to be impractical. The French consultants did not have the means to lead a project of this magnitude and were too far away from the statue, the contractors, the suppliers, and the National Park Service. There was also the language barrier. Except for Grandjean, no one in the *groupement* spoke English.

Though having a binational team resulted in more broadly based decisions, the effort of conducting meetings and following conversations in two languages was exhausting.

Other cultural differences gave those meetings much of their dimension and color. In Paris, meetings were conducted in rooms soon filled with black Gauloise smoke, and meals were always lengthy and serious affairs with plenty of good food, wine, and amiable conversation. In New York, sandwiches were served, and smokers were asked to refrain from indulging in their habit. The American members were more often than not irritated by the formal and lengthy presentations of their French colleagues, while the French at times resented the Americans' more direct, give-and-take form of discussion. In the end, the challenge of the project would always get everyone through the argument at hand. We remember the early meetings with great fondness.

Nevertheless, misunderstandings and communication breakdowns did happen. The French had been expected to prepare a draft diagnostic report for review and discussion. Three weeks before a formal presentation to the Park Service, Grandjean arrived instead with the initial fifty copies of a complete, printed report. It was beautifully laid out and illustrated. Unfortunately, many sentences were awkward, there was a usage problem, and ignorance of American sensitivities was often apparent. More important, the report presented unsubstantiated

In New York, 1984.

Foundation: The Statue of Liberty–Ellis Island Foundation, Inc., is a not-for-profit corporation chartered in the state of Delaware to raise funds and undertake the restoration of the Statue of Liberty and Ellis Island. It is chaired by Lee A. Iacocca. William May is the president and Stephen Breganti and Robert Cahill are executive vice presidents.

At dawn (facing page).

theories that would not have been acceptable to the fact-oriented National Park Service.

The report needed to be completely rewritten. The American members had little time to prepare the revision and had the added burden of diplomatically explaining this decision to their French colleagues.

Meanwhile, the French-American Committee was having difficulty in raising funds. By contrast, the Statue of Liberty–Ellis Island Foundation was gaining momentum. The foundation, established in 1981, worked in liaison with the Statue of Liberty–Ellis Island Centennial Commission, created by President Ronald Reagan. Under the leadership of Lee A. Iacocca, who is credited with rescuing Chrysler Corporation from bankruptcy, the foundation was raising funds from the American people for the restoration of the Statue of Liberty and Ellis Island.

As the foundation's list of donors grew, so did its concern for a timely completion of the design work. The foundation, responsible for the construction phase of the project, would have liked to assume responsibility for the design phase as well.

Some jurisdictional problems developed. The French-American Committee felt strongly that as it had initiated the statue project and its

10

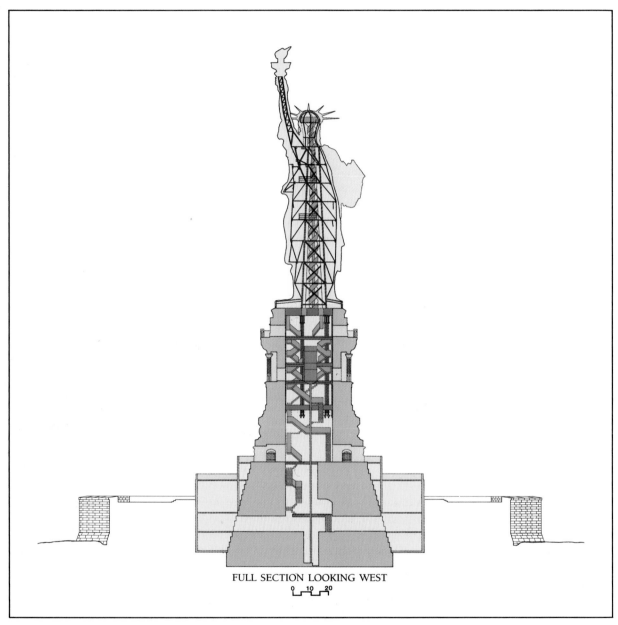

FULL SECTION LOOKING WEST

0   10   20

Section of the monument.

12

Commission: The Statue of Liberty–Ellis Island Centennial Commission is the federally approved advisory body to the U.S. Department of the Interior and its National Park Service for the centennial restorations of the two historic sites.

groupement had alerted Americans to how badly deteriorated the statue really was, the committee should retain control of the design phase. Moreover, the National Park Service insisted on leaving control of the design work in the hands of the committee to ensure a clear separation of responsibilities.

During 1982, the growing involvement of the Park Service effectively made some of its representatives members of the design team. Blaine Cliver, chief historical architect of the North Atlantic region, was assigned to the project.

Cliver brought with him an acute sensitivity for preservation and insisted on the thorough and scientific analysis of historical facts with proper documentation of alternative solutions. His serious attitude as a historical architect and his experience in classical archaeological digs served the project well. It was largely due to his efforts that the National Park Service and the Department of the Interior accepted such a comprehensive restoration. At times, however, Cliver's championship of preservationist issues would bring him into conflict with the design team.

The Park Service's superintendent, David Moffitt, also contributed to the project. Moffitt had lived on Liberty Island for many years and knew the statue better than anyone else. During the early period, he attended many working sessions, offering his experience and insight regarding the statue's management and always remaining the advocate of the handicapped and the elderly. Garnett Chapin, special assistant to the directors of the National Park Service, was another who devoted considerable energy to the department's goals.

Despite the informal relationship we enjoyed with Cliver and Moffitt, the design team was required to make formal presentations to them and other government officials at critical stages in the project. In July 1983, the diagnostic report having been completed, a formal presentation to Russell Dickenson, then director of the National Park Service, was made in Washington, D.C., followed by a press conference.

For this presentation, Jean-Pierre Tissier, son of Tissier the elder, had built an 8-foot 4-inch (2.5-meter) metal model of the statue's framework. The work was full of detail, from its central pylon down to its gusset plates.

Moments before the press conference, the model was discovered to have been damaged in transit. Last-minute repair attempts damaged it further. Hoping that no one would notice the missing pieces, the design team moved the incomplete model into the presentation room. It was well received, and the press conference was a great success, with national television, radio, and newspaper coverage. However, Jean-Pierre Tissier was extremely upset over the "sabotage" of his masterpiece, and this incident added to the tension between the French and American participants.

By the fall of 1983, the team was struggling to get the design phase in full swing; the CETIM engineers instrumented the statue and set up on the island to record the statue's vital signs. However, the U.S. Customs Service and the winds were not cooperative. Some of the instruments sent from France were detained at the airport, and the normal winds of the fall season, so necessary to some of the more important measurements, did not materialize. Moreover, in Paris the significance of July 4, 1986, was not always recognized, and the urgency of the schedule was not perceived by the French colleagues.

Owing in part to lack of funds from the French-American Committee and its unfamiliarity with American standards and requirements, the French team members were simply not producing their share of work. The American team kept receiving incomplete sketches when full-drawn details were needed, narrative documents instead of technical reports, and speculative theories in lieu of solid historical or scientific analyses of verifiable data.

13

By December 1983, concerned that the project would incur the same delays as the original construction project a century earlier, we decided the American team had to take a stronger role in the project. From that time on the roles were reversed, with the Americans taking responsibility for the design phase and the French *groupement* serving as consultants.

Given the realities of the schedule, the *groupement* reluctantly accepted this change of responsibility. The French-American Committee for its part, funds still lacking, was all too happy to see the project moving forward. The National Park Service, though concerned that the sensitivity brought to the project by some of the French members would be lost, recognized the need for this reversal of roles.

The decision to assume design leadership for the project required expanding the American group. Robert Landsman of Swanke Hayden Connell was brought in as a full-time project director. Landsman is an experienced architect with a good design sense combined with strong managerial ability. He very quickly learned of the complexity of the binational team relationships, which he came to describe as similar to the relationship between Roosevelt and De Gaulle in World War II.

Edward Cohen was asked to increase his involvement and to bring in Ammann & Whitney to take on structural as well as mechanical and

Study model of the statue's structure, 8 feet 4 inches (2.5 meters).

electrical design responsibilities. To further support the team, Howard Brandston Lighting Design, Inc., was retained as lighting consultant; John A. Van Deusen and Associates, Inc., as elevator consultant; Vito Cerami, as acoustician; and Geod Surveys, as surveyor.

A committee of objective design professionals was established to review the work and make alternative recommendations. Swanke was asked to organize this group. George White, the architect of the Capitol, accepted the chairmanship of the Architectural Advisory Committee. White's experience in monumental architecture and his acute sense of responsibility as an officer of the United States government made him well suited to the task of chairman.

Concurrently, the National Park Service reinforced its team by assigning John Robbins as project architect. Extremely precise, thorough, and meticulous, he was soon totally devoted to the demands of the project.

The foundation's first project director was Ross Holland, formerly with the National Park Service. Holland brought an understanding of Park Service goals as well as the foundation's concern for schedule and budgeting.

To support Holland, the foundation had retained E. Lawrence Bellante, partner in the firm of GSGSB Architects Engineers Planners. Bellante first served as staff engineer and later as the foundation's project director for the restoration project.

Bellante, a former fighter pilot, has a no-nonsense approach to work as well as an insistence on impeccable professional work standards. Many times when conflicts arose with the foundation over an important design issue, Bellante was skillful in diplomatically and effectively calming the waters. During the construction phase, when time and budget constraints became most acute, Bellante proved to be a tireless and very effective project director.

As the tempo of the project increased and work progressed, tension continued mounting with the French colleagues. Just when the American team thought that it had finally resolved the differences in work habits and organizational problems, it ran into more substantive disagreements over some of the core issues of the project.

The issue of preservation became especially divisive. The French, surrounded at home by centuries-old buildings, had a broader historical perspective and a rather more casual approach to the restoration of a structure "barely" 100 years old. This cultural bias was compounded by differences in approaches to problem solving. The *groupement* had a tendency, on the basis of preliminary information, to formulate theories quickly and draw conclusions to be tested later. The American design team was reluctant to draw conclusions before assembling a complete collection of information. This difference in attitude kept dividing the participants on specific issues.

In retrospect, Moutard's intuitive grasp of the statue's behavior based on his lifelong experience as a master craftsman proved in several instances to be as perceptive and appropriate as our time-consuming and sometimes ill-fitted insistence on a scientific approach. Modern technological processes are not always applicable to problems of a craftsmanship nature. This was true with the copper repoussé work, the forming of the armature bars, and the gilding of the flame. The design team came to this realization only later in the project when work was in progress. By then, Moutard was no longer part of the team.

The statue had to be a fast-tracked job, and construction was to get under way well before the final design documents were complete. For this, late in 1983, credentials were requested from a number of construction firms, and with the team's recommendation the foundation selected Lehrer/McGovern, Inc., as the construction manager with Eugene McGovern as the principal in charge. His commanding and sometimes intimidating manner serves him well in a tough industry. His

Years of planning were finally becoming a reality (overleaf).

16

Restoration photographer Dan Cornish.

Jacques Moutard (left) and Pierre Tissier (right) studying an armature-bar replica.

17

knowledge of construction and his skill in obtaining performance and resolving fractious disputes were brought to bear upon the job.

Philip Kleiner became Lehrer/McGovern's project manager, and George Hoehl was responsible for the project schedule. Later on, Jay Gang assumed the challenging role of the on-site construction supervisor.

By the spring of 1984, bid packages for construction were being issued. At the same time, the scope of work kept expanding. The National Park Service asked the design team to renovate the statue's pedestal and started discussions concerning a Statue of Liberty museum at the base of the pedestal.

Meanwhile, the French-American Committee's fund-raising problems had worsened. The lack of funds was now threatening the project itself, for it was by then evident that the committee could not fulfill its commitments.

Consequently, the American design team terminated its contract with the committee in August 1984. We had made this difficult decision during a walk in the garden at Versailles. It was a memorable morning. In the fog and drizzle, the garden had a consuming effect on us. It helped put things back into perspective. We resolved that regardless of amicable ties and the historical precedent of joint French and

From left: Pettibone, Gang, Callahan, Bellante, Despont, McGovern, Cahill, Kleiner, Peters, and Robbins.

American involvement, the issue had to be settled with the committee to ensure the completion of the project on time.

The foundation immediately assured the American team that it would welcome its continuing involvement. With National Park Service concurrence, Swanke Hayden Connell signed a new contract with the foundation to continue its role as architect for the restoration of the Statue of Liberty with the Office of Thierry W. Despont as associate architect and Ammann & Whitney as structural and mechanical engineer.

Unfortunately, the French consultants' own contractual arrangements with the French-American Committee and a dispute with the foundation over fees led to the termination of their involvement. The differences aside, we regretted the end of the collaboration—the growing friendships, the inspired ideas, the long workdays, and the debates.

But there was little time to look back. The large team of architects, designers, and drafters at work in our offices under the direction of Dominic Scali was producing the more than 200 drawings needed for the restoration. Shortly thereafter, the decision was made to proceed with the Statue of Liberty museum, a significant project in itself, which deepened everyone's involvement and required an even larger team.

Construction was in full swing by the fall of 1984. Three years of planning were finally becoming reality: the scaffold wrapping the statue was up, the torch was down and being replicated, the armature replacement was under way, and the skin was being cleaned.

During construction, the brunt of the effort fell to the construction manager's team, the foundation staff, and the Park Service personnel. Kleiner and Gang, Lehrer/McGovern's construction site supervisor, Bellante and his staff, and Cliver and Robbins were all working days and nights under the watchful eye of Robert Cahill, the foundation's executive vice president. Weathering all storms, real and imaginary, they managed to complete this by then enormous project on time.

To ensure the project's conformance with the design documents, members of the team had to visit the statue many times and spend countless hours in coordination meetings. But no matter how often we all boarded the construction boat, it was with great enthusiasm and expectation.

When the time came for the project to end and the team to be dismantled, we knew we would remain united by our memories and by all that had been accomplished.

We had become the veterans of Liberty.

RESEARCH

*At the view of the harbor of New York, the definite plan
was first clear to my eyes . . . in the pearly radiance of a
beautiful morning is revealed the magnificent spectacle of
those immense cities, of those rivers extending as far as
the eye can reach. . . . In this very place shall be raised
the Statue of Liberty, grand as the idea which it embodies,
radiant upon the two worlds.*

FRÉDÉRIC-AUGUSTE BARTHOLDI
*Sculptor
from "The Statue of Liberty
Enlightening the World," 1885*

Bartholdi's true genius resides in his vision upon first entering
New York harbor: his selection of Bedloe's Island as the site for
the statue was and remains flawless.

As Bartholdi saw the harbor, so it is today. The mornings still have
the same pearly radiance, the immense cities offer an even more magnificent spectacle, and the rivers are still endless to the eye. Going to and
from the statue, one is struck by the beauty of the harbor and exhilarated by the Manhattan skyline, whether it is basking in the early-
morning sun, reflecting the glory of the sunset, or aglitter in the night.
The majesty of the bridges, the grace of the ships still move us. The
tantalizing power of the elements, whether one is shrouded in fog,
sprayed by mist, or blown by the winds, is a welcome greeting when
departing the everyday world and heading for the statue.

It is a wonder that the creators of the Statue of Liberty could have
accomplished their dream, exacting in its design, execution, and assembly even by today's standards. Their achievement is our inherit-
ance.

As the latter-day colleagues of Bartholdi, Eiffel, and Richard Morris Hunt, the American architect for the pedestal, our job was merely to
finish the work they began more than 100 years ago. To restore the
statue properly, we had to be thoroughly familiar with the thoughts of
her creators.

Our reaction to the harbor helped us. We still feel as Bartholdi felt,
see as he saw, and sense what he sensed about the ultimate significance
of his work enhanced by its setting. The harbor is part of our common
experience—an experience that transcends time.

With the achievements of the statue's creators, we have also inherited their limitations. Though the general concepts for the statue and

*The torch and flame in Monduit/Gaget, Gau-
thier et Cie workshop, Paris, 1876.*

21

"At the view of the harbor. . . ."

her framework stood the test of a century, nature's elements and millions of visitors had aged her considerably.

Like archaeologists we studied in minute detail all aspects of the original construction and of subsequent transformations of the statue. As we progressed, we encountered many ghosts. Some were less than welcome. The statue had been changed—and sections even mutilated—by those charged with protecting and maintaining her over the years. But this too is part of her history, and we had to decide which sections should be kept and which discarded. Should Bartholdi's and Eiffel's original work or even intent be restored and given primacy over subsequent transformations, or should the historical wear and tear be preserved?

This question struck at the heart of our work. Unfortunately, there were no easy answers. Much of the statue's history was and remains a mystery. Even after exhaustive searches, no single repository for documents describing the original construction and subsequent changes could be found. The statue's documented history was piecemeal at best and scattered all over the world, in obscure books and magazine articles, in public museums and private collections.

We had Bartholdi's notes and correspondence but no detailed drawings. Some of Eiffel's calculations and sketches were available, but nothing revealed his attitude toward the structure built at variance with his original design. We consulted Hunt's drawings but had to deal with an incomplete and greatly modified pedestal. Interpretation thus became a major part of our work.

Bartholdi wrote his thoughts and reflections in a journal in 1885, when the statue was completed in Paris. By then he was an established sculptor. Born on August 2, 1834, in Colmar, a city in the Alsace region of France, he was raised in Paris. As a young man, he studied architecture with Eugène-Emmanuel Viollet-le-Duc, the foremost architect-restorationist of his time, and painting and sculpture with Ary Scheffer. By his early twenties, he had begun his lifelong obsession with colossal and monumental works.

Sculptor Frédéric-Auguste Bartholdi.

Engineer Alexandre-Gustave Eiffel.

23

*Original drawings: Eiffel's surviving draw-
ings show the framing of the central tower
and the upraised arm and do not include the
secondary or tertiary framework and details
of the connections. Eiffel's wind-force calculations were available to the team. We did not
find Bartholdi's or Gaget, Gauthier's fabrication drawings. A patent drawing by Bartholdi
has survived.*

*Our insistence—and that of the National
Park Service—on complete files and documents throughout the centennial restoration
project was a concerted effort to ensure that a
detailed record of the centennial restoration
would be preserved for future reference.*

In 1856, he went to Egypt to study ancient works. He returned to Cairo in 1869 to propose creating a monumental sculpture for a lighthouse at the entrance to the Suez Canal in the form of a woman holding a beacon.

In 1871, Bartholdi made his first trip to the United States and upon entering New York harbor he had his vision. The Statue of Liberty would be a colossal sculpture of a woman holding a torch in her upraised arm, sited on Bedloe's Island.

Back in France, Bartholdi developed a series of small clay models showing figures of Liberty in different poses and attitudes. Having refined his concept, he presented it to the French-American Union, received its support, and set out to build the statue.

He was familiar with the seventeenth-century statue of St. Carlo Borromeo by G. B. Crespi, a 76-foot- (23.2-meter-) high sculpture in repoussé copper over an iron armature, built on Lago Maggiore near Arona, Italy. Bartholdi had visited this statue upon his return from Egypt. He also knew of the statue of Vercingetorix by Aimé Millet built by the Etablissement Monduit, the predecessor of Gaget, Gauthier & Cie, the firm that would build the Statue of Liberty. Vercingetorix was also of repoussé copper, with an iron armature designed by Viollet-le-Duc. The restoration of this statue a century later raised the question of whether the Statue of Liberty was similarly in need of help and began the process that would call international attention to her poor state of health.

Bartholdi selected copper for his sculpture, as cast bronze or stone would have been too expensive and too heavy to transport. He asked his former teacher Viollet-le-Duc, twenty years his senior, to design the statue's structure and skin-attachment system.

Viollet-le-Duc proposed supporting the 151-foot- (46-meter-) tall figure with masonry compartments filled with sand. This giant pile was to rise only to the hips. Above that, he planned a lightweight system of construction.

He proposed an armature system of iron bars to support the copper envelope like veins of a leaf, based on the system he had previously

used on the Vercingetorix statue. It is unclear how he intended to
connect the armature to the masonry.

One hundred years later, the restoration team would retrace Bartholdi's initial investigation and visit the statues of St. Carlo Borromeo
and Vercingetorix.

Viollet-le-Duc died in 1879 before most of the figure had been
built. We presume that only his design for the iron head arches had by
then been executed. Though there are no records to confirm this, none
of Eiffel's subsequent drawings show the head framing. Also, the head
was exhibited at the Paris International Fair of 1878, ten years before
the body of the statue was completed.

Soon after Viollet-le-Duc's death, Bartholdi approached Eiffel,
who at forty-seven years old was his contemporary and well known for
his long-span iron bridges. Eiffel, who would soon achieve world fame
for the Eiffel Tower, was a daring, brilliant engineer with revolutionary
design ideas.

His approach to the framework was radically different from Viollet-le-Duc's. Eiffel utilized and adapted concepts developed for his
bridge designs and proposed a central iron tower for the statue's pri-

Returning from the statue.

25

mary support. This was a major departure from traditional masonry-bearing-wall structures of the period.

Eiffel's other most original contribution to the design of the statue was the system of flat bars or springs that connect the armature system inherited from Viollet-le-Duc to the secondary structure that emanates like a tailor's mannequin from the primary structure. Those bars allow the skin-support system to behave independently of the primary and secondary structures while transferring gravity and wind-induced loads to these structures. The inventiveness of such a system is impressive.

The decision to keep Viollet-le-Duc's skin-attachment system, which placed dissimilar metals in contact, would plague the statue and provide the primary impetus for the centennial restoration. Copper and iron, in the presence of moisture, produce an electrolytic reaction that causes the iron to corrode and eventually disintegrate. Eiffel anticipated this and tried to prevent it by isolating the metals. This only delayed the corrosion. Moreover, examination revealed that asbestos material had been used as insulation. The restoration work would be complicated by this fact.

Eiffel's superb calculations withstood both the test of time and our subsequent computer-aided analysis. His design remains as brilliant today as it was 100 years ago.

To fully understand the design for the structure and its behavior under wind forces, the CETIM technicians recommended the installation of 142 strain and acceleration gauges. This instrumentation furnished crucial information about the structural behavior of the statue and provided the necessary data to evaluate Eiffel's original calculations.

Though Eiffel borrowed the concept used to support the statue's figure from bridge technology, nothing previously had been done on such a large scale with an enclosed structure. At 151 feet (46 meters), the statue would be the largest of the existing colossi, and standing on a 154-foot (46.9-meter) pedestal, it would be the tallest structure ever built in its day. Solving problems of scale and calculating the compression, expansion, contraction, uplift, and sway resulting from wind loads and storms were relatively new and untried disciplines, especially for an exposed harbor location.

During the diagnostic phase of the project, we discovered to our surprise that the head is offset some 2 feet (0.6 meter) and the shoulder framing approximately 18 inches (45.7 centimeters) from the axis of the central tower, in defiance of Eiffel's drawings. This answered one question (why the framing was weak) but raised others: why, when, and who made the change? Two years of painstaking examination of historic photographs established that the change had been made during assembly in Paris, not in New York.

Until then, hours were spent speculating, each member of the team adopting and defending a theory: the change had been made to accommodate Bartholdi's artistic eye; the change was the result of compounded misalignment during assembly either in Paris or in New York. There was agreement on only one thing: Eiffel had had no part in this modification. Its clumsiness departs from the overall elegance of his structures. Unanswered questions aside, the method to remedy the dis-

The largest of the existing colossi.

tressed shoulder became one of the main subjects of debate during the project.

For his part, Bartholdi completed and refined clay models of increasing scale. In the workshop of Gaget, Gauthier, artisans built full-size plaster fragments from Bartholdi's one-third-scale models. Over 100,000 individual measurements were taken while building the separate sections of the statue.

Wooden framing beneath the plaster supported each section. The plastic models were refined under Bartholdi's guidance until he gave final approval. In his journal he says: "After this last enlargement changes were no longer possible. Now the sculptor could only aim at very great precision, and at great care in the modeling of the surfaces, which were becoming enormous." Old photographs show the sculptors covered with plaster from head to foot standing beside the large pieces.

Negative wooden forms reversing the model's contours were then built. By using the repoussé technique, the copper sheets were hammered against the mold on the reverse side of the material. In this way, workers shaped the some 300 individual copper plates for the figure. Once the figure was completed, temporary bracing kept the shapes from becoming distorted. Holes for the rivets that would connect the plates to each other were then punched. Only one out of every ten rivets was installed when the figure was assembled temporarily in Paris.

One hundred years later exactly the same process was used to replace the torch and flame. Time spent studying history had proved valuable.

Sections of the statue were first erected in Gaget, Gauthier's workshop. It was a startling scene. In one vintage photograph (see page 20), the right hand holding the torch and flame takes center stage, dwarfing workers around it. Models of varying size give the scene an extra dimension. Faces in bas-relief on a mural watch over the activity. In the almost surreal photograph, the lines blur between art and reality.

Full-size plaster model in Gaget, Gauthier et Cie workshop, Paris, 1883.

Building the statue in Paris.

29

In 1882, assembly work began on the entire figure in the shop's courtyard. The statue soon towered over the buildings of Paris and became a curiosity for Sunday strollers in the Parc Monceau.

Workers first erected the iron skeleton, including the box truss for the upraised arm. Using a light wooden exterior scaffold and the skeleton itself for access, they started attaching the skin from the bottom up.

By 1876, the torch and flame and a portion of the arm had been completed and sent to the Philadelphia Centennial Exposition, where they were a popular attraction. Later they were sent to New York and remained on display at Madison Square Park until they were shipped back to Paris in 1883.

A comparison of photographs taken of the flame in the United States and after it was returned to Paris in 1883 revealed that one of the flares had been altered radically and relocated so that it then projected away from the main body of the flame. Here again we are left to speculate as to the reason for such a change: aesthetic considerations of the artist finally seeing his work 151 feet in the air or a crude construction requirement to provide a hole centered on top to attach lifting cables within for assembly?

We like to think such a major change was directed by Bartholdi himself and for no other reason than aesthetics. He did appear to have several changes of heart with regard to the flame—the replica on the Seine, built under his supervision, has a remarkably different shape.

The flare modification was the first of many changes to the flame over the years. Subsequent ones, however, were made in the United States and not authorized by Bartholdi. They plagued the statue as well as the centennial restoration.

By the spring of 1885, when the statue was packed in 210 crates and ready to leave for America, it was nine years late. Funds had been in tight supply and construction more demanding than anticipated. Then, after its arrival in the United States, it remained in crates until the summer of 1886. Work on the pedestal was the responsibility of the Americans, and it also was delayed by lack of funds and construction problems.

Flame in Paris before modification, 1884.

Flame after modification in New York, 1885.

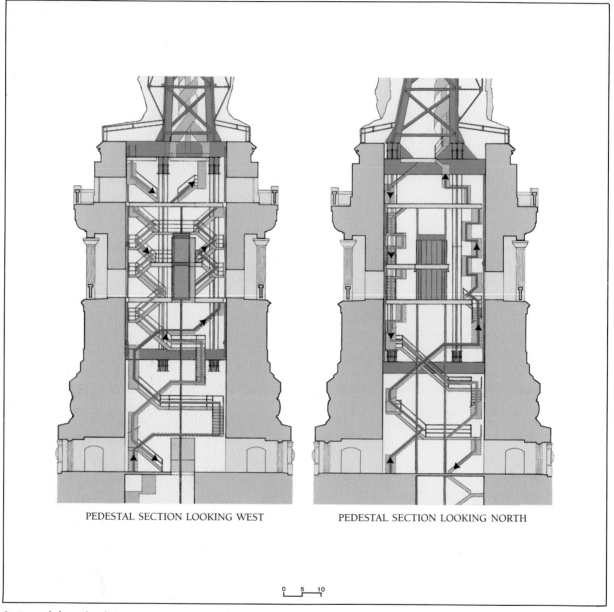

PEDESTAL SECTION LOOKING WEST   PEDESTAL SECTION LOOKING NORTH

0   5   10

Sections of the pedestal.

32

Pedestal architect Richard Morris Hunt shared Bartholdi's sympathy for Egyptian monumental art. He even named his pedestal studies *Pharos I* and *Pharos II*. However, their relationship was not always smooth. In 1885, Hunt was in Paris with his family for an extended stay and failed to contact Bartholdi, much to the sculptor's disappointment.

Hunt was a flamboyant society architect. He was fascinated by French culture and was the first American architect to be trained at the Ecole Nationale des Beaux-Arts. There, he honed a considerable talent to design mansions in the Beaux-Arts style. Hunt's long list of credits includes several Newport great houses and summer "cottages" for the Vanderbilts and others and many fashionable houses along Fifth Avenue in New York.

Hunt's pedestal design took into account sketches made earlier by Bartholdi. The Hunt drawings were studied in developing our proposal for the renovation of the pedestal, and the concept for visitor circulation reflects the order of his original design.

The final design for the pedestal called for a gradually tapering 114-foot- (34.7-meter-) tall tower, covered in granite, sitting on a broad foundation with rusticated stone. A Doric socle near the bottom, a surrounding balcony near the top, and a colonnade section on each face directly below the balcony break the massive form. The tower

Construction of the pedestal, Bedloe's Island, 1885.

height was subsequently reduced to the existing 89 feet (27.1 meters), sitting on its 65-foot- (19.8-meter-) tall stepped foundation.

Though the pedestal is tall and is broader than the statue, it enhances rather than detracts from the sculpture. Investigations during the restoration revealed that the axis of the central pylon is not positioned directly over the axis of the pedestal. Its placement is based upon the golden-ratio system of proportions, a guiding principle frequently used in classical architecture to ensure elegance. The same ratio was used in designing the new stair system within the pedestal.

General Charles Pomeroy Stone, U.S. Army engineer, directed the construction of the pedestal. Ground breaking took place in April 1883. Excavation work got under way that June, and the laying of the foundation began the following October. Work then continued until December of the next year. In May 1885, it started again and was completed in October 1886. The granite came from a quarry on Leete's Island in Connecticut.

During the summer of 1886, after waiting fifteen months for its pedestal, the statue was finally uncrated and reassembled by a team of French and American workers. Here, the restoration parallels and contrasts with the original construction. During both efforts, the island location posed problems of logistics, including getting workers and materials to and from the site and being somewhat at the mercy of the tides and the weather. But modern technology's advantages of power and speed made the restoration work much simpler in many respects.

In America, the statue was assembled in completed levels from the inside out. The workers attached the skin to the self-supporting frame as it rose instead of building the entire frame first and then attaching the skin from the bottom up, as was done in Paris. Derricks hung off the central pylon. Workers standing on the structure would lean over the edges of the skin's copper plates to install the rivets. An exterior scaffold was not necessary.

The restoration effort required an elaborate scaffold. Every square inch of the exterior envelope had to be accessible to examine its condition, clean it, peen the rivets, and repair the cracks. When designing the scaffold, we looked with envy at the lithe and elegant wooden one

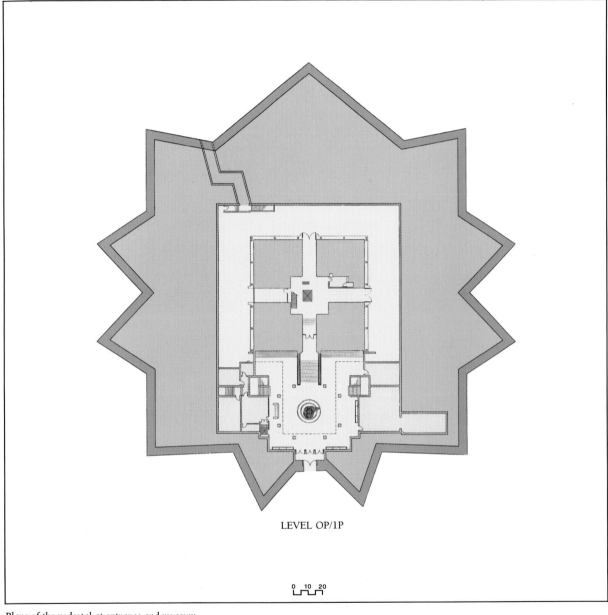

LEVEL OP/1P

0 10 20

*Plans of the pedestal at entrance and museum
levels.*

Restoration:

"Restoration: to restore an edifice. It is not to maintain, repair or rebuild it, it is to reestablish it in a complete state which may never have existed at any given time." (Viollet-le-Duc, Dictionary, 1854–1868.)

"Restoration . . . stops where hypothesis begins: beyond that any additional work needed is part of architectural creation and will bear the mark of its time." (Article 9 of the Charter of Venice, 1964.)

Differences in attitudes toward restoration have never been resolved (probably never will be). They are subject to the sociological outlook as well as the technological capabilities of the time.

built by Gaget, Gauthier for the assembly in Paris. Environmental conditions and safety regulations forced us to design a much more elaborate system.

In 1886, Bartholdi recommended that lights be placed on the torch platform to cast a strong light on the flame while leaving the gilded copper intact. The plan then prepared called for eight lamps with reflectors. This idea was changed only a week before the inauguration by a U.S. Army Corps of Engineers expert employed to install the lighting, who argued that the strong lights would dazzle ships' pilots navigating the harbor.

The flame was modified by cutting two rows of portholes and installing lights within. Perhaps it was thought that Liberty should be lighting the world instead of enlightening it! But the results were more than disappointing. Observers onshore in Manhattan at the dedication ceremony on October 28, 1886, could hardly see the light from the island. Bartholdi was appalled and quoted as saying that the flame gave off the "light of a glowworm."

The disappointing glow aside, Bartholdi's spirits were high on the inauguration day, which was filled with pomp, fireworks, and speeches. It was Bartholdi's proudest moment: his dream had become reality, and all the world was watching. "You are the greatest man in America today," President Grover Cleveland told him.

History has it that Monsieur Gaget had come to attend the inaugural ceremonies, bringing with him three large trunks filled with miniature replicas of the statue stamped Gaget, Gauthier. As those miniatures grew in popularity, so did an Americanized form of his name. "Gadget" soon became a household word.

The original makers of the statue could not have realized what changes lay in store for her over the years. The flame was again modified in 1892, as everyone agreed that the portholes were a dismal failure. To improve the lighting, an 18-inch- (45.7-centimeter-) high belt of glass replaced the upper row of circular windows, and an octagonal pyramidal skylight with red, white, and yellow glass was installed on top of the flame. This distorted the shape. On seeing it in 1893 during his last trip to the United States, Bartholdi was again disappointed.

The crowning blow to the original flame came in 1916, twelve years after Bartholdi's death. Gutzon Borglum, the sculptor of Mount Rushmore, resculpted the flame into a lantern of some 250 panes of amber glass in a copper grid. For the upper half, he simply cut the grid out of the original repoussé copper. For the lower half, he installed new copper, as the original had already been removed for the portholes and the glass belt.

This change mutilated the original flame inside and out. The flame began to take water and triggered the corrosion that would eventually require the replacement of the entire torch. With today's preservationist attitude, it is difficult to imagine allowing anyone to tamper with the design of a national landmark, as Borglum was permitted to do.

Research into the history of the flame and documentation of its changes were essential in determining how to replace it.

Other major alterations to the interior of the statue had been made to accommodate an ever-increasing flow of visitors. Curiously enough, it seems that Bartholdi did not intend the statue to be open to the public. The finishes were rough, and an original wooden stair was provided for maintenance workers only. This is surprising, for Bartholdi held several celebration dinners in the statue in Paris and comments approvingly in his journal on the beauty of the interior.

On the day of its inauguration, the statue was open to the public in response to popular demand and has remained open ever since. The familiar double-spiral stair was built in Brooklyn and installed for visitors climbing to the top. Later, an elevator and stairs were installed in the pedestal, and still later a museum was added at the base. At each

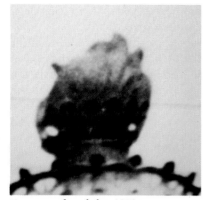

Two rows of portholes, 1886.

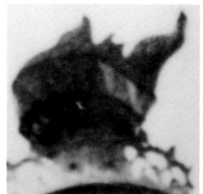

The band of glazing, 1892.

Borglum lantern, 1916.

Helical stair with protective screens.

change, however, plans were made more in response to pressing need than in fulfillment of any long-term master plan.

In 1936, the National Park Service organized a restoration effort that, though limited in scope, recognized the main physical ailments of the Statue and tried to stem their tide. Armature corrosion was on top of the list. The work was only a stopgap measure, however. Like the original metal, the replacement bars were iron.

The lack of exterior scaffolding was a major limitation to the work. Because of this, self-tapping screws, not rivets, were used in repairing the skin-attachment system.

The inherent problem of corrosion, covered by layers of paint, grew to gigantic proportions before being recognized. The irony is that Bartholdi thought this would never happen: "In regard to the preservation of the work, since all the elements of its construction are everywhere visible on the inside in all their details, it will be easily kept in good condition." He did not foresee regular painting of the interior.

The statue would have to wait until its centennial restoration for an overall program to be developed to improve the circuit of the visit and expose to the visitors the beauty of its interior. Before we could proceed with this task, however, we had to re-create a complete set of

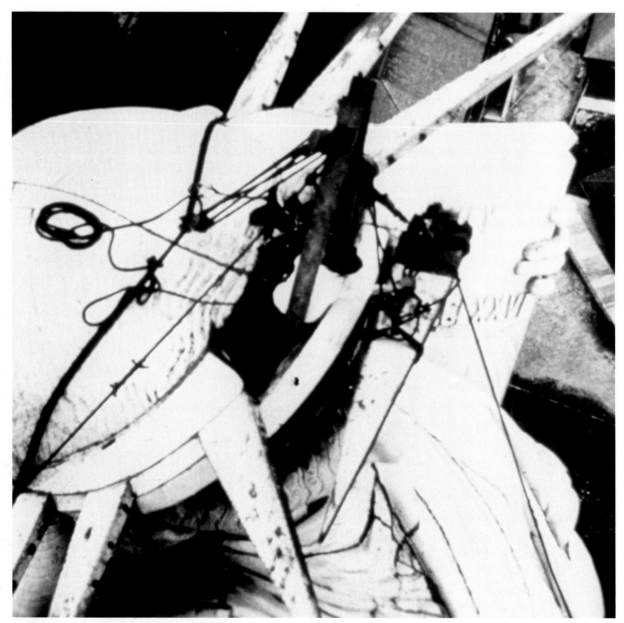

Restoring the spikes, 1936.

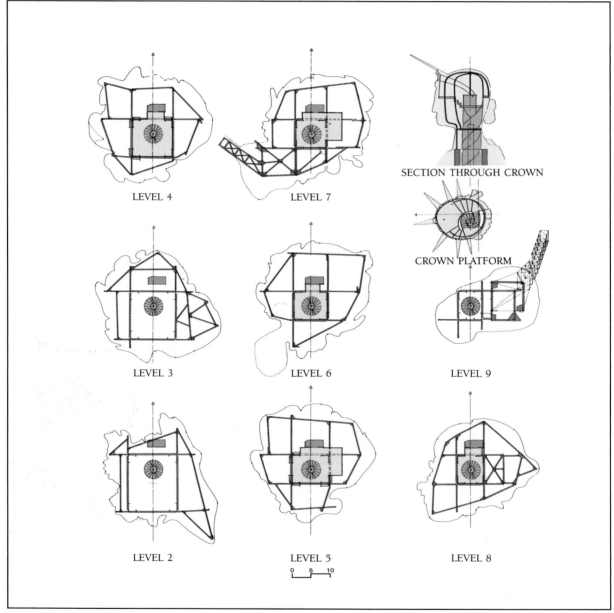

LEVEL 4

LEVEL 7

SECTION THROUGH CROWN

CROWN PLATFORM

LEVEL 3

LEVEL 6

LEVEL 9

LEVEL 2

LEVEL 5

LEVEL 8

0 5 10

Plans of the statue at various levels.

(Top) Eiffel wind-load diagram; (below) computer representations of the statue.

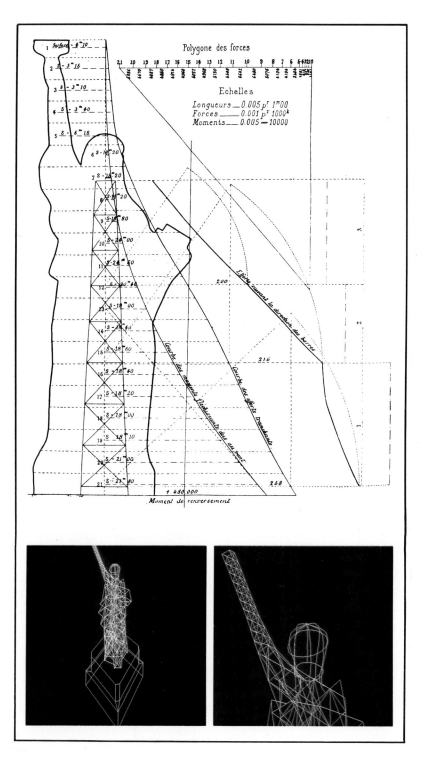

architectural, structural, mechanical, and electrical drawings. We did this while studying the statue's history and getting to know her creators. With all the information gathered, we could diagnose her condition and decide on treatment.

Computers simplified and expedited the task of creating new drawings. We plotted the measurements of the primary and secondary structures into our system to develop a graphic representation in three dimensions and in color. This process saved time and allowed a visual understanding of how the structure is articulated. It helped orient everyone on the design team to the interior, which was not easy to perceive while winding up the spiral stair within the screened central pylon.

Like Bartholdi, we built models. Every element, down to the gusset plates, was measured, scaled, and represented.

41

After the drawings and models had been completed, a series of measurements were made to gather environmental data. This helped discern the movement of air outside and within the statue and the levels of carbon dioxide and moisture present. It was crucial to complete our knowledge regarding the statue's behavior and response to environmental conditions.

Data from the environmental survey, collected for an entire year, were sent by computer to the Park Service office in Boston and to Paris. Samples for testing the composition of the copper and iron were also taken and the patina analyzed. X-ray analysis was used to verify that there were no hidden cracks in the structure.

After two years of intensive investigation, we felt that we not only knew the statue's characteristics and ailments but understood the thinking of her creators.

At last, we were ready to begin the work!

SCULPTURE

Colossal statuary calls for faculties of particular power. It is an art of an exceptional character which presents considerable difficulties. Conception and execution are controlled by rigid and difficult laws. Faults once committed can be hidden by no subterfuge, and if the artist fails, the depth of his fall is commensurate with the immensity of his aspirations.

CHARLES BLANC,
Critic
Le Temps, *1884*

Bartholdi set out to create a colossal, conservative, and timeless statue. He gave it the figure of a classically draped woman holding a torch in her raised right hand and a tablet in her left. With her left foot she steps on the broken shackles of tyranny. The right leg, in a classical contrapposto pose, is set back so that the figure seems to be advancing when viewed from the side but looks stationary from the front. Her face is rather austere. On her head is a crown with seven spikes, representing the seven continents and seas of the enlightened world.

Like Bartholdi, architects experience similar challenges in designing buildings. We must deal with size and scale long before ground breaking, build models to study forms, and have confidence in our judgment long before a building has been completed.

Bartholdi had a unique opportunity to modify the statue when it was erected in Paris. It was probably then that he moved the shoulder and modified the flame.

Bartholdi knew what qualities were called for in colossal sculpture: "I may cite for example the principle of great simplicity in the movement and in the exterior lines. The gesture ought to be made plain by the profile to all senses. The details of the lines ought not to arrest the eye. The breaks in the lines should be bold, and such as are suggested by the general design."

These are basic characteristics of good architectural design. From afar, there is coherence. Closer, order becomes apparent. At human scale, details are revealed.

Historically, in most cathedrals and monumental stone buildings, the best masons were used for work at the base and apprentices fin-

A colossal sculpture and her scaffold, 1984.

45

"Great simplicity in the movement and in the exterior lines. . . ."

ished areas farther from the eye. The statue's detail, however, is consistent in quality throughout. Her lines are strong and clear. There is great beauty in the detail—the fingers, the torch, the face.

To be successful, colossal statuary must produce a strong emotion. Bartholdi succeeded at this in the statue and perhaps in his other large work, the *Lion of Belfort,* but even they owe their success to size and quality of execution rather than to innovative subject and form. Bartholdi had not only the talent but the drive and the fortitude to give reality to his grandiose dreams. He was an average sculptor in the prevailing neoclassical style of his time when dealing with ordinary-size forms. If not for the statue, Bartholdi would be little known today.

Like Lilliputians confronting Gulliver, we had to gain access to the giant statue. A scaffold was required to wrap such a gigantic piece of art. A concept was needed to surround her without harming her, to withstand the "hundred-year" storm and to leave intact her fragile green patina.

We could neither remove sheets of copper nor pierce the skin. We had not yet determined the structural capacity of the framework. Because of our concern about overloading the existing structure, the design had to be completely independent of the sculpture itself—a free-standing system equal to the statue in strength, for if it failed, the potential for damage to the statue would be enormous. We considered several concepts. One involved cables anchored to the ground. Another was to build a pyramid around the statue.

The cable concept was eliminated because long cables vibrate in the wind and would in turn have vibrated the scaffold, making work impossible. Under such conditions, workers would either get "seasick" or lose weight.

The selected scaffold system began at the base of the pedestal and rose more than 300 feet (91.4 meters) above the island. It was belted around the base at four levels with tension ties. The upper 150 feet

Scaffold: It took four months to erect the scaffold, early in 1984. Made of heavy-duty aluminum tubes, the scaffold was prefabricated into frames that were then "stitched" together in the field by using additional horizontal members and X bracing. In plan, the system formed an 81-foot (24.7-meter) square. The scaffold's four corner towers took all lateral loads. The structure was designed to withstand winds as high as 100 miles per hour. It was supported at four levels on the pedestal through double aluminum channels in compression butted against the pedestal's corners. Tension ties—cables—belted the pedestal at each of the four levels. During the passage of Hurricane Gloria on September 27, 1985, the strongest gust of wind recorded at the top of the scaffold was 73 miles per hour without adverse effect to the scaffold or the statue.

(45.7 meters) never touched the copper envelope of the statue itself. This giant vertical cantilever was kept at a distance of approximately 18 inches (45.7 centimeters) from every part of the statue to allow for movement under strong winds. Portable work platforms were moved from one area to another to give workers closer access to the skin when necessary.

The system was designed to support the arm in place structurally should a decision be made to detach the entire arm to repair the weakened shoulder. It was also designed to support a derrick boom to remove the torch and flame.

The scaffold was engineered and installed by Universal Builders Supply, Inc. This unorthodox "workshop" cost about $2 million. Fittingly enough, some of the system components were fabricated under licensing rights of a French patent.

Common scaffolds are made of steel components. Here, aluminum was selected, for even painted ferrous metal would rust in the salty harbor environment and drip onto the statue, harming the copper patina. This concern had led us at one point to consider a bamboo scaffold with nylon strapping, common in the far east.

Access was required over the wall of Fort Wood, which surrounds the pedestal and is considerably broader than the base of the statue. The use of one elevator alongside the fort and another alongside the scaffold was ruled out. Running two hoists and transferring workers and materials back and forth would have been impractical.

A *blondin*—a cable-and-hopper system commonly used in France—was considered. Like a ski lift, it would begin at the edge of the island and rise up at a shallow angle to the scaffold. Its ingenuity notwithstanding, the concept ran aground when safety regulations were taken into account.

Instead, a 400-foot- (121.9-meter-) long ramp was built over the fort to the base of the pedestal. There, a hoist rose the height of the scaffold in an area adjacent to the torch and flame. The ramp, consist-

47

. . . closer, . . .

. . . and at human scale.

ing of wooden planks on steel scaffolding, was designed to carry a loaded truck or even a mobile crane.

To provide entry from the scaffold to the statue during the work, we considered removing several plates of the copper envelope, in particular ones at the sole of the right foot used for entry 100 years ago. Other entry points on the statue would have been more direct and convenient, but the concern to protect the skin prevailed. In the end, the pedestal balcony doors were used.

Our anticipation and excitement grew as we watched the scaffold rise during the first months of 1984. It was erected during the winter so that work could begin on the exterior that spring. Unusually harsh weather conditions made this work very difficult. But the statue's spirit had already captured the workers' imagination, and a race was on among the scaffold erectors to see who would be the first to give her a kiss on the lips. At the first kiss, the weather improved. It was a good omen.

Before the installation of a hoist, we would climb the scaffold stairs and walk the bars of this giant jungle gym, carried by our enthusiasm at finally being able to draw close and touch the statue.

The scaffold crew took more than the usual pride in its accomplishment. At their unofficial topping-out ceremony—a party in a local

Like Lilliputians.

49

Access ramp over Fort Wood.

Contrapposto.

51

bar on Wall Street—they expressed the kinds of emotions we had been feeling ever since the beginning of the project. What a joyous and exhausted group! It was a privilege and a pleasure to be with them at that moment.

The next day, April 27, 1984, was the official topping-out ceremony at the statue. Everyone was buoyant. It was an occasion we had dreamed about for three years.

From afar, the scaffold added mystery to the statue. It wrapped her like a protective cocoon, a lacy web that let her show through in vague profile. On the scaffold, the magnificent details of the sculpture were revealed. At long last, members of the restoration team were able to pour over the statue as only Bartholdi and his workers had been able to do.

The excitement of rising alongside the statue in the construction hoist rivaled the early-morning boat rides. Arriving at the top, 300 feet (91.4 meters) in the air, we would be greeted by her upraised arm, Manhattan in all its glory as a backdrop, and the world around us in miniature. Under strong wind, the scaffold sang to us. It had a life of its own. The experience was eerie yet exhilarating.

The hoist ride was so stirring that George White suggested installing another hoist for the public, and Garnett Chapin asked us to study the idea. After reviewing it without success with elevator contractors, we consulted Ferris-wheel operators, but there were too many problems, safety regulations aside. Any temporary elevator, limited by size and capacity, would not have been able to move visitors in a timely manner.

Close examination of the copper skin could now be done at all times of the day. As the sun moves across the southern sky, the shadows change on the statue, as do the colors, emphasizing the folds of the copper envelope and revealing the different shapes and lines of the sculptural form.

Many surprises awaited us: from bird nests to graffiti, from torn rivets to hidden cracks. The copper skin was surveyed in detail and small samples taken for laboratory analysis. To complement our work, GSGSB was asked to photograph the entire statue, plate by plate.

Built of red copper, the statue had turned a tawny brown by its inauguration. Then, it began to develop its familiar green color as it underwent patination, a natural change that occurs when copper is exposed to moist air. Bartholdi intended this to happen—he thought it would make the statue look more like a classical bronze sculpture.

Cliver took on the added responsibility of studying the chemical makeup of the patina, hoping not only to deal with its protection but also to draw conclusions on many of the characteristics of patina for future restoration work.

Ultrasonic calipers, instruments that would not mar the surface or harm the copper, were used to measure the thickness of the skin. The

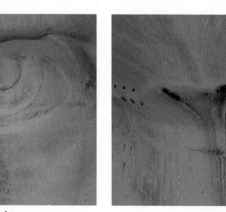 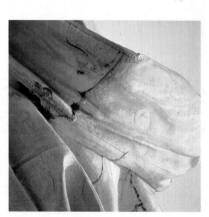

Details of the copper skin.

A protective cocoon . . .

. . . a lacy web.

53

technique of repoussé by its nature results in material of varying thickness. The measurements confirmed that the existing copper skin was generally the original thickness of 2 millimeters, or about ³/₃₂ of an inch thick—the thickness of a penny.

The skin was in relatively good condition, other than in discrete areas where tearing or cracking had occurred and on the torch and the flame. We were asked repeatedly throughout the restoration whether the exterior would be cleaned and the patina removed. The answer was a resounding "No!" Quite the opposite, we went to great lengths to protect and preserve it. The uniformly developed patina, which had protected the copper from corrosion and deterioration, would allow the copper to weather several hundred years more.

With the questions came suggestions from many quarters regarding what to do or not to do to the outside of the statue. One letter from a child asked us for a piece of the statue, "no bigger than a desk," so that his class could conduct an experiment: "We will drop it into the Hudson River to see if it turns green, although I don't know how we will get it back."

Despite its generally clean condition, the statue had many stains. While some looked ugly close up, from afar they blended into the overall texture.

Some of these stains were streaks of coal tar and paint that had oozed from the interior through the statue's seams. Paint had been accidentally dropped on the back of the arm from the torch balcony. And a dark area on her back was probably caused by smoke from the island's trash incinerator.

Birds like the statue as much as people do. Many built nests in the draped folds of the robe. In some spots, a century of bird droppings had turned into a solid block of material, detrimental to the copper and very difficult to remove.

Different methods of stain removal were tested: metal scrapers, microscopic-glass blasting, chemical solvents, and liquid nitrogen. Some simply didn't work, and others would have removed the adjacent patina as well as the stain. None of the methods tried proved to be either efficient or practical. In the final analysis, it was decided to

Curl damaged . . .

Cracks in the statue's nose and chin (over-leaf).

pressure-wash the entire statue and carefully scrape away only those stains and bird droppings visually and chemically detrimental to the statue.

Next, cracks, tears, and blemishes were tackled. The most numerous were dimples and stretch marks caused by rivets that had pulled away. They were also the easiest to repair. While the armature was being replaced, new prepatinized rivets were installed using the existing holes. In the process, the copper was gently hammered to soften the most obvious dimpling.

Of more serious concern were some large cracks, tears, and missing pieces encountered at various points: cracks in the statue's right eye, lips, and chin; a damaged nostril, a missing hair curl; badly patched plate assemblies at complex folds; and broken foot chains found completely detached from the statue. We were especially surprised at the size of the cracks on the statue's nose and chin. Those unsightly scars had more often than not been retouched on published photographs of the statue.

The cracks were repaired. Large ones were patched by using the traditional "wolf-mouth" assembly. For the most serious ones, like the nostril, a mold was taken of the original part and a replacement repoussé piece prepared. Minor tears were simply hammered back together and sealed from the inside.

Carved names and other graffiti dating as far back as 1886 were left. Two of our favorites were an engraved *B* for Bartholdi on the first copper plate to be riveted and "Alone with God and the statue, Christmas Eve," on the big toe. Names were even found in the middle of the statue's back, scribbled by workers lowered down in baskets from the torch platform during the 1936 restoration.

Proper weep holes were installed to allow condensation to escape from the interior of the statue's deep horizontal folds.

The armature framework within the crown spikes had deteriorated. The spikes were brought down to be cleaned and the armature replaced. The outside edge was found to be bronze and the top and bottom brass, not copper. Again, the lack of complete records on the

. . . and repaired, 1985.

original project and subsequent alterations kept haunting us. Were the brass and bronze spikes original or replacements? Was the bronze used for a structural cantilever? Stamped numbers on the pieces, similar to the stamping on the copper plates, showed them to be original. The bronze and brass were probably used because they were stiffer than copper and the spikes needed the extra strength to cantilever from the head.

One of the spikes of the crown was in contact with the upraised right arm, probably because of the sway resulting from the displaced and weakened shoulder. It was easier to move the spikes than the arm. So the spike position was adjusted by a few degrees to gain clearance.

Not all the problems encountered in repairing and cleaning the skin predate the restoration project; some were caused by it. Despite the preparatory testing on samples and exacting specifications there were occasional surprises.

Early one morning, we received an urgent call to come to the statue. She was turning blue! When we arrived, Robbins was already there, attempting to neutralize the inappropriate, however beautiful, hue.

The culprit was carbonate crystals formed by rainwater and sodium bicarbonate, a mild abrasive powder used to remove the coal tar from the inside surface of the copper. Careful attempts to contain it had failed, and the fine powder had leaked through cracks in the fingers near the stub of the removed torch. Rainfall caused a chemical reaction that produced the carbonate.

The entire area had to be rinsed with heavy volumes of water as the bright blue crystal, if left long enough on the patina, would actually microscopically explode and push the patina off the surface. The rinsing and rain showers eventually returned the statue to its natural green color.

By the time the restoration began, the statue was barely carrying her torch. During one of the first visits, a photograph was taken of the two of us with park rangers on the torch balcony. When this photograph was shown at the next team meeting, we were advised not to

Crown spike in contact with right arm.

A precarious situation: torch pendant inside (top) and out (below) before restoration.

58

attempt this "daring feat" again. In the opinion of our distinguished colleagues, the armature of the torch was seriously weakened.

As our study progressed, we realized that, although not about to fail immediately, the torch and flame indeed required complete replacement. The uppermost tip of the monument was actually sending out a distress signal by waving in the wind. As Bob Hope said at one of the fund-raising events: "I knew she was in trouble when I waved to her and she waved back to me."

The torch was the part of the statue most exposed and battered by the elements. The balustrade, made of a thinner-gauge copper because it has intricate ornaments, was in terrible shape.

The most serious structural damage, however, was caused by water leaking in through the flame of the poorly sealed Borglum lantern with its 250 pieces of glass. Water and a mixture of bird droppings and other organic deposits had leaked into the handle of the torch and accumulated at the bottom in its acorn-shaped pendant, forming a kind of primordial soup. A short time ago, a threaded rod had been inserted with a large bolt into the bottom of the pendant. If not for that, the pendant would have fallen off. Curiously, the same piece was missing from the replica on the Seine, and we supplied the restorers in Paris with an exact drawing to aid in its replacement.

Most of the pendant was salvaged, but the armature had to be replaced. It had completely disintegrated! Only a line of demarcation remained where it once was.

It would have been futile to try to patch the existing torch and flame as it was so badly deteriorated.

How would the torch be replaced? Should it be made to resemble the original or its most recent version? We were inclined to restore the flame, not preserve it. Without hesitation, we pushed aside the concept of the Borglum lantern, for it had been a mistake in the first place. Actually, the shape was dreadful, so dreadful that we fondly dubbed it the "ugly teapot."

Exhaustive research on the successive transformations of the flame and replacement alternatives followed. Replacement by a single piece of blown or cast glass in the shape of the original flame was

59

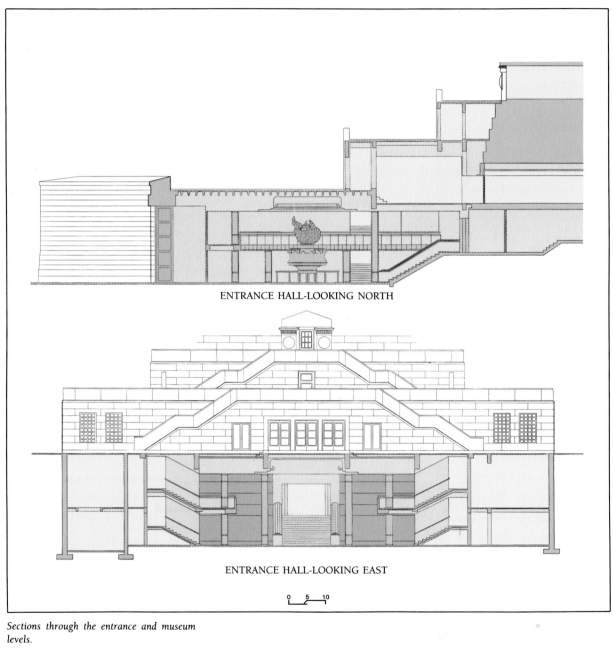

ENTRANCE HALL-LOOKING NORTH

ENTRANCE HALL-LOOKING EAST

0   5   10

*Sections through the entrance and museum
levels.*

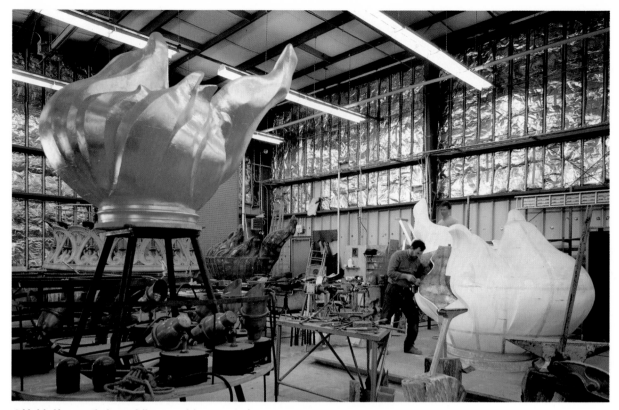

Gilded half-size and plaster full-size models in restoration workshop, 1985.

rejected because either process is extremely difficult to accomplish without cracking the glass. Also, the completed flame would have weighed five to seven times more than the existing flame, necessitating a redesign of the already weak shoulder framing. Production problems, potential breakage, and the need to store replacement pieces also eliminated a solution using large pieces of glass. Pieces of heat-formed acrylic or an equivalent synthetic material would have solved the breakage problem but introduced others: sagging during manufacture, high expansion and contraction when in place, and deterioration under prolonged exposure to the sun.

Our final recommendation was to replicate Bartholdi's original gilded-copper flame. It was then decided to preserve and display the Borglum lantern in the statue's museum.

Duplicating the original shape became a major challenge as little information existed about it. The existing flame was so distorted that it could be used only as a guide. Not only had the bottom sagged, the original repoussé copper on the lower half had been lost in the Borglum transformation.

Based upon historic photographs gathered by Carole Perrault of the Park Service and our team, one-twelfth-scale clay models of the flame were made. The number of flares that were on the original was identified by piecing together the different photographs.

Plaster casts were then made from the clay models, in much the same way as Bartholdi had worked in sculpting the flame. We worked with models as an artist would with a sketch, refining the scale and proportion.

To replicate the torch and flame, artisans were needed who could handle ornamental and sculptural copper repoussé much as it had been handled a century ago. Despite 100 years of technology and new construction techniques, the original method of construction—the crafts approach—was still the best. Finding such a contractor wasn't easy. Today, repoussé is a little-used technique.

In concert with the construction manager, the foundation, and the Park Service, a search began. Twenty-four bids were received. This number was narrowed to twelve—eight from the United States, two

61

Making the mold for the new flame (and facing page).

from France, and one each from Germany and the United Kingdom. In the end, the French firm Métalliers Champenois was selected, and a team of twelve artisans led by Serge Pascal and Jean Wiart came to build the new flame on the island.

The work on the torch replica could not begin without removing the existing one from the statue. This was done during a public ceremony on July 4, 1984. It represented another milestone for the project, and we were filled with emotion as the torch was lowered.

In a workshop built near the base of the statue, the removed torch was set on a work platform. There, the French artisans could reach its many pieces to measure it and prepare the molds for its replacement.

A half-scale plaster model of the flame was developed. To ensure the correct shape, the existing but distorted flame was measured and machine-cut plywood slats piled up to form the general contour of the flame. The plywood base was covered with plaster, and historic photographs were used as guides to modify the shape.

Computers helped us again. Photographs of the flame and the model were digitized and drawings produced of the existing flame and the mock-up to the same scale. The drawings were superimposed and the two shapes compared in utmost detail (See Plates XVIII and XIX).

This state-of-the-art tool helped pick up areas of discrepancy between the old flame and the model and allowed us to proceed with the full-size plaster mock-up. Throughout this process, a measurement every 0.79 inch (2 centimeters) was obtained to establish 4000 reference points on the flame.

With only several views shown on old and blurred photographs, it was difficult to verify the angles and shapes. One could not tell how sharp were the original edges, how gradual the curves.

Then a full-sized plaster model was prepared. For months, advising the French artisans as Bartholdi must have done, we added, chipped, removed, and added again until the shape was finally approved.

Next, the artisans divided the surface into twenty-five segments based on the number and shape of copper plates originally used. Small pieces of sheet metal were fitted together to cover the final model like a knight in armor. These pieces were spot-welded to form a mold. Exterior bracing and concrete were added to reinforce it. The copper was then hammered against the interior surface of the mold.

The formed sections of copper were overlapped and riveted. Joints were smoothed and soldered to fill in any gaps that could cause the still-to-be-applied gilding to crack.

63

We debated at length gilding the copper flame by electroplating or gold leafing. In electroplating, the gold is bonded to the copper by an electrolytic reaction, either by dipping or by brushing. This produces a smooth surface and can last for decades. Gold leafing consists of applying very thin sheets of gold onto a surface. After exhaustive testing, gold leafing was selected for its luminescent quality, its beauty, and its historical accuracy as well as its durability. For the flame, the copper had to be coated with an organic material to insulate it from the gold. Then, a resin had to be applied that received the gold leaf.

To replicate the balcony, a series of detailed drawings was developed to prepare the required tin forms. Original pieces were copied very precisely. The Park Service located a piece of the original corncob ornament from the balustrade in the National Archives in Washington. A plaster cast was made from it.

Repoussé, especially for intricate pieces, requires very gentle hammering and extraordinary craftsmanship. There is always the danger of cracking the material.

As the work proceeded, more debates on restoration and preservation concerning the many details of the torch followed. One centered on the two layers of decking found on the platform floor.

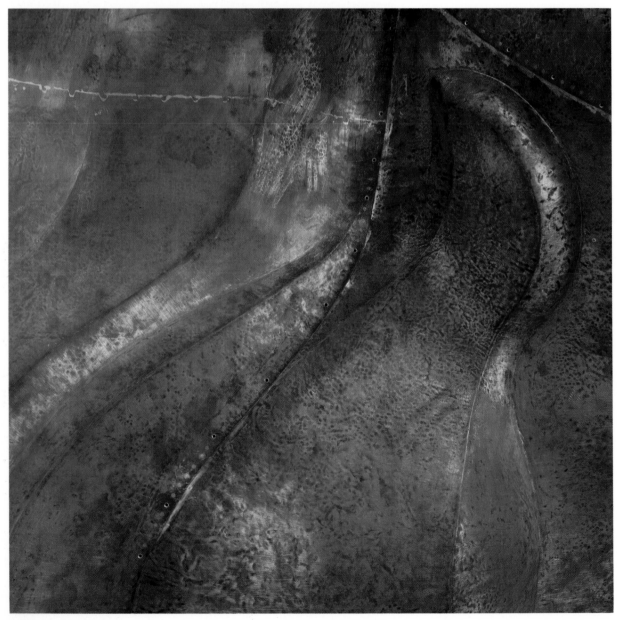

Respoussé.

*The authors with Howard Brandston (left)
and John Robbins (right) at test-lighting
mock-up of the gilded flame.*

Gold-leafing the flame, 1985.

65

The original fluted layer, which thousands walked upon in Philadelphia and then in New York for the several years the torch was displayed, showed signs of wear from the number of visitors. At some point, either in Paris or when the statue was first erected in New York, a new deck was added. Should one or two layers be installed in the replication? To remain true to the original, only one deck was used.

Below the torch platform, a series of oval openings follows the reverse curve of the torch drum as it narrows to become the handle of the torch baton. These openings were probably for ventilation. Differential pressure between the exterior and the interior on the statue would suck water into the statue during storms. The design was modified to correct the problem and bird screens added to limit the number of uninvited guests.

Finally, lighting the flame required special attention. In Bartholdi's mind, the statue was first and foremost a sculpture, not a lighthouse. However, the symbolism of a flame burning for liberty demanded that it shine as brightly as ever for all the world to see.

The half-scale gilded mock-up was employed for lighting tests. Using projectors on the torch balcony and in lighting pits on the ground, the flame was set ablaze. With today's lighting technology, the flame can be as bright and intense as one may wish. Bartholdi's original intention and the dreams of those wanting to see a burning torch in the night have finally been reconciled.

The overall lighting concept, developed with consultant Howard Brandston, was designed to provide drama and reinforce the sculptural qualities of the monument. The fort is lit softly, the pedestal a bit more brightly, the hem of the robe even more. Gradually, the level of illumination is increased again and again, culminating with the brightest intensity at the crown and torch.

The intent is to enhance and reveal the statue's sculpture and composition in the harbor setting. Rather than as an overpowering hulk rising mysteriously from the sea, the statue appears with grace and distinction.

The level of lighting is tuned to highlight certain details. On the pedestal, the recesses at the colonnade level are backlit to provide a

67

The flame alight in the harbor.

The flame completed and installed.

Tools and the task.

Metal halide lamp: Metal halide lamps are highly efficient lamps in which rare metals are partially vaporized in an arc tube to produce light in a color range that can be controlled. Working with General Electric's research laboratory, two different-colored metal halide lamps were developed. Their Kelvin temperatures were fine-tuned to enhance the green-patina coloration and accentuate the sculptural details. For the gilded flame, incandescent lamps were used.

strong and bright light source within the vertical slots, emphasizing the fine proportions.

To refine the lighting design, the statue was used as a full-size mock-up in a series of night tests. Views from various spots on the island, in the harbor, and from buildings in Manhattan and nearby roads and bridges were studied. The illumination intensity was recorded and compared with the existing lighting installed in 1976 for the United States bicentennial.

A powerful xenon portable torchlight was used during those tests. It was so strong that from the tip of Manhattan one could direct the light and pinpoint it onto the flame or the face. On the statue, it was used to indicate the precise effect of shadows resulting from direct and indirect lighting.

Different gradations of blue, green, and white light were tested to obtain the proper color, warmth, and distinction. Those evenings spent testing the lighting are among our most memorable. We felt exhilarated while illuminating the statue, changing its aspect almost at will. Like a modern-day Prometheus, for a few moments we brought to her fire and light.

With the lighting completed, there was only one major element of the exterior that needed attention. The statue did not have a proper

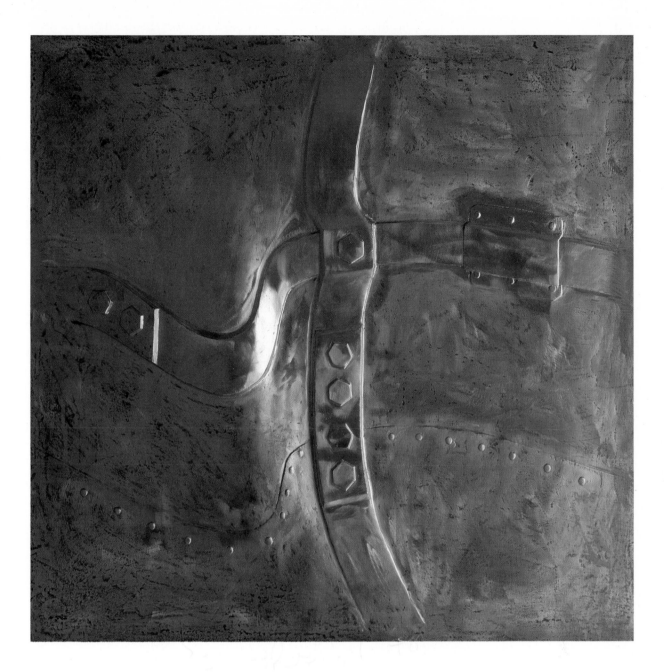

The centennial doors: Cast in bronze in the best artisan's tradition, the panels depict the tasks and the tools of the centennial restoration. From top to bottom and left to right they represent:

Left side
  Panel 1 Copper repoussé
  Panel 2 Scaffolding
  Panel 3 Tools: Electricians, plumbers, and mechanics
  Panel 4 Armature
  Panel 5 Stonework

Right side
  Panel 1 Tools: Carpenters, metal workers, painters, and finishers
  Panel 2 Refurbished helical stair
  Panel 3 Structural repair at shoulder
  Panel 4 Visitors' elevator
  Panel 5 Tools: Architects, engineers, and surveyors

entrance. If the torch and flame were our passion during the restoration, so became the entrance doors during the renovation.

Since 1960, access to the statue had been through a mediocre set of utilitarian doors within the walls of the star-shaped fort. Clearly the millions of visitors to the statue deserved a dignified and welcoming entrance.

The 1960s entrance was removed and an opening 21 feet (6.4 meters) high and 9 feet (2.7 meters) wide rescaled within the massive rusticated walls. We designed a pair of monumental doors to fill the opening and provide an imposing portal to the statue. The centennial doors are made of bronze, with ten bas-relief panels crafted with the help of Jordan Steckyl's skillful hands. They tell the story of the statue's construction and centennial restoration through the work of the artisans and the tools of their trades. As visitors pass through, they will be reminded of the dedication and spirit of the thousands who labored on the sculpture.

STRUCTURE

*Some walls are mute, some talk, and some others, the
most beautiful ones, sing.*

PAUL VALÉRY,
Poet and Philosopher
from Eupalinos, or the Architect, 1932

The monument's interior was full of unexploited potential. Hiding behind protective "prison" screens, platforms, and poor lighting was a structural wonder, a cavernous space crying out to be unleashed.

The centennial restoration did more than restore the statue's sculpture and framework to health, it exposed its marvelous structure. Our early visits to the statue interior were spent exploring, looking, and feeling. It was then that the seeds were planted for our drive to unveil the structure. In those early days of discovery, we were like archaeologists stumbling onto treasure after treasure.

The initial program from the Park Service asked that the visit be made safer, more secure, and environmentally comfortable for the some 1,500,000 people who pass through the monument each year. But the program had to be expanded to embrace the spirit, please the senses, and stimulate the mind.

One by one, earlier alterations had chopped up the original volumes, making the sensible incomprehensible. This jumble of failed spaces—intimidating, mysterious, and rather dizzying—was returned to its original unobstructed state and the visit reorganized to offer views and vistas never before possible. Visitors had always been so preoccupied with the climb that they rarely stopped to look around.

As our journey of discovery continued, the need to provide some clarity and direction to the public became apparent. The visit was confusing and disorienting, as though one had to go through a warehouse to see the Taj Mahal. Instead, a direct, new, clear, and more stimulating tour was developed. Visitors now orient themselves by keeping sight of the monument's interior. New lighting retains the mystery and revives the grandeur.

The structure itself had to be repaired. The iron armature that connects the skin to the framework was the most badly decayed. When the statue was first surveyed, almost 30 percent of the riveted saddles that attach the armature network to the copper envelope were found to be loose or damaged. The asbestos isolator had disintegrated, and in many areas the iron armature bars had swelled with rust. This swelling consumed the space between the saddles and the bars, thereby restrain-

The monument's interior.

73

A jumble of failed spaces.

Skeleton: The statue's skeleton has three main components. The primary framing is a central pylon or tower—a vertical truss made of angles and plates that are triangulated for stiffness. The secondary framing is also triangulated and consists of light angles. The tertiary system is the skin-support and attachment system. It is made of rectangular bars that form a grid against the interior of the copper envelope. The bars are about 6 feet (1.8 meters) long, are bolted together, and are bent to conform to the folds of the copper envelope. The bars are connected indirectly to the envelope by riveted copper saddles. The connection allows the copper skin to move independently of the armature as they each expand and contract in response to changes in temperature caused by the sun's daily movement across the statue. The armature is connected to the secondary framing by a system of flat bars and springs. This gives the skin a "living" frame that responds to the external pressures of the wind and transfers these loads to the secondary and primary frames.

ing the flexible sliding joint. The skin-attachment system became overstressed, and in many cases the swelling and pressure caused rivets either to shear off or to rip out. Rainwater then began leaking through the open rivet holes, accelerating the decaying process. If left unattended, the envelope would eventually have collapsed.

The many coats of paint applied to the interior kept the corrosion hidden from view and aggravated it by trapping water underneath. In places, the thick paint was the only material holding together a section of almost completely disintegrated armature bar.

The damage was so extensive that the entire armature system, including rivets, saddles, and flat bars, had to be replaced.

The selection of a replacement material for the armature brought forth again the issue of preservation versus restoration. Should it be iron as the original material or a material more compatible with copper on the galvanic scale?

If, to satisfy the preservationist point of view, iron were selected again, in time the same rampant corrosion problems would occur. A list of criteria that any replacement material would have to satisfy was developed. Prime among those was the restoration concern not to unbalance a complex support system that had worked well for years. This meant a metal similar to iron physically, structurally, and visually.

A red-copper alloy would have virtually eliminated the problem of electrolytic reaction and been easy to form into the complex shapes of the armature bars. But larger sections would have been required to achieve the same strength as iron, greatly increasing the armature weight.

Evaluations were made of different alloys of stainless steel, composite materials, and copper-plated metals. But time was not available to develop exotic composite materials, and the plating would not withstand abrasion.

Cliver, working with Norman Nielsen, a metallurgist consultant to the Park Service, recommended ferallium, a high-strength alloy of steel and aluminum used by the British Navy as a bronze substitute. Nielsen indicated that ferallium would substantially reduce the galvanic reaction and would have weight and stiffness similar to those of iron.

74

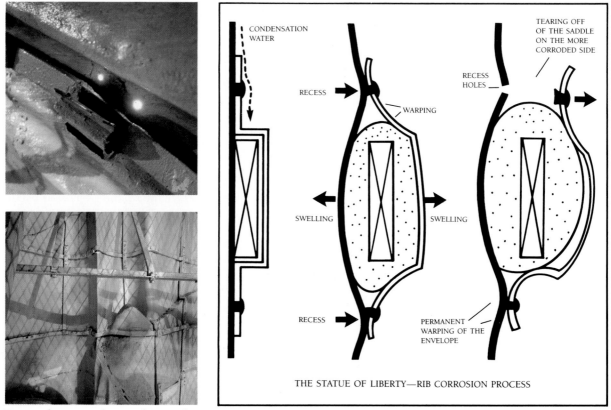

Process of armature decay and its results.

CONDENSATION WATER

RECESS

WARPING

SWELLING

SWELLING

RECESS

PERMANENT WARPING OF THE ENVELOPE

TEARING OFF OF THE SADDLE ON THE MORE CORRODED SIDE

RECESS HOLES

THE STATUE OF LIBERTY—RIB CORROSION PROCESS

Making an armature-bar template.

Armature-bar-replacement sequence: Several methods of duplication were considered, including making molds of the original and computer-aided photogrammetry. This involved digitizing the measurements and sculpting the bars by robotics. The molds were rejected because they would have had to be very rigid to shape the stainless steel. Field conditions made photogrammetry impractical.

The bars were removed and duplicated by first making a template of the original and then using the template to form the new bar. The bending of the bar caused work hardening. The bar then had to be annealed to relieve the resulting stresses. This was done by heating with an electrode attached at each end. The glowing red bar was then quenched in water. After annealing, the bar had to be sandblasted to give it a uniform finish. Then the bar had to be passivated, dipped in a nitric acid bath, to bring back the oxide protective coating. The removal, reshaping, and replacement sequence had to be accomplished in a maximum of thirty-six hours to maintain the continuity of the armature network at all times.

However, ferallium was very difficult to shape, primarily because of its tendency to bounce back. Stainless steel 316L, a low-carbon, low-corrosion material, was then considered and found easier to bend. The material could be used in bars of the same cross section as the original iron bars. The stiffness characteristics of the system would be similar, and the rivet holes could be reused.

In the final analysis, stainless steel 316L best satisfied the criteria and was selected for the armature bars. Ferallium was chosen for the flat bars owing to its springlike quality.

An isolator was still required between the stainless-steel bars and the copper skin and saddles to avoid the risk of galvanic reaction under extreme conditions. Inducing an electric current into the entire system to balance the flow of ions and neutralize the reaction was considered. Ultimately, Teflon tape with pressure-sensitive silicone backing was selected as the isolator.

Before replacing the armature, the entire system of some 1825 individually shaped bars, 325 springs, 2000 saddles, and 12,000 rivets had to be surveyed and delineated to define the scope of the work. A technique for duplicating the bars also had to be devised.

Various high-tech duplication approaches were considered, but a traditional crafts-oriented method was deemed best. A template for each replacement would be made by an artisan using a soft metal. This template would then be used in the workshop to form the new bars to the same profile.

The scope of the work and the schedule required that modern production technology be combined with traditional craftsmanship. No single firm could be found with such capability. A joint venture was formed between Nab Construction, a large steel fabricator, and P. A. Fiebiger, a third-generation metal workshop with a tradition of European craftsmanship. Nab/Fiebiger was awarded the contract for the replacement of the armature, one of the most difficult undertakings of the restoration.

An elaborate bracing system had to be designed to ensure that no movement of the skin or armature would occur while bars were being replaced. Any small amount of movement could lead to a disaster by causing the skin to be torn or badly deformed. A rigorous removal sequence was established, dividing the statue into quadrants and limiting the number and location of bars that could be replaced at the same time.

The presence of asbestos, discovered in the Eiffel isolation material, complicated the procedure. Workers had to don white protective suits with their own air supply and special arrangements made to dispose of the asbestos. The crews in their "moon suits" were reminiscent of a NASA launching operation and gave the entire operation a look of otherworldliness.

Upon removal, the bars were stripped of paint and asbestos. Next, they were duplicated by using heat and forming presses at the workshop on the island or in Fiebiger's shop in Manhattan. After annealing and passivation, the new bars were installed.

The stainless-steel replacement material had arrived at the site covered with rust. This superficial corrosion was caused by iron machinery used in fabrication. The rust had to be removed, if only for aesthetic reasons.

Installing temporary bracing and tying off the bars, stripping the asbestos and paint, bending and shaping the new bars, replacing, and riveting had to be done within thirty-six hours to maintain the schedule and limit the risk of distortion of the skin. This was no small feat, considering the individual shape of each bar and the complexity of the replacement procedure for a trip off the island.

Bellante used his engineering experience and management skills to develop a precise and lengthy procedure manual specifying step-by-step removal and replacement instructions.

Armature bracing covered with sodium bicar-
bonate.

At several critical points during the twenty-five-step procedure, the work was inspected and rejected if necessary. In full production, workers were able to replace seventy bars each week, laboring twenty-four hours a day. The removed bars were used for fund raising through their sale as memorabilia—gadgets.

New copper saddles were fabricated to match the old ones. New conical rivets were ordered, some to match the rivets being removed and replaced, others to fit through the enlarged holes made by the rivets that had pulled away from the skin. The conical shape allowed the rivets to fit within the various sizes of holes without causing any tearing or buckling of the copper skin. The heads of the rivets were prepatinized so that the statue would not appear as though she had chicken pox—red-copper rivet heads against the existing green patina.

The next most serious condition within the structure was the displaced and weakened right shoulder. Whatever the reason for the displacement, from a structural standpoint the modification of Eiffel's original design was incorrect. The connection of the right arm to the pylon was eccentric, too flexible, and overstressed. There was a lack of continuity in the joints. This allowed twisting and excessive

77

movement. Previous repairs had compounded rather than solved the problem.

The design team was confronted with the decision to repair or replace the shoulder framing. It proved to be one of the most difficult philosophical and structural dilemmas of the project, pitting restorationists against preservationists, French against Americans, engineers against engineers. We recommended returning the framing to the structurally and visually more elegant Eiffel design. Cliver wanted to keep the original bracing and any subsequent reinforcement, even if inadequate, as a historical record.

Over a period of more than twelve months, tests and designs were prepared for replacement and repair schemes. We had to be satisfied that either scheme would be structurally sound. CETIM engineers and Lehigh University used computers to simulate local and general behavior of the statue for each alternative.

When the engineers finally resolved their differences and produced designs of equal structural soundness for both solutions, the Park Service insisted that the shoulder be repaired rather than replaced. Structural elegance is not necessarily appealing to architectural historians.

Model of the monument.

The constant twisting of the arm over the years had raised another and potentially more serious question: Was the entire iron framework suffering from metal fatigue? A piece of the original puddled iron, a French relative of wrought iron, was removed and sent to be tested.

Ironically, the very cause for concern turned out to be a characteristic that had helped the statue withstand the vicissitudes of time. The iron was soft and had inclusions and impurities. The imperfections gave it an extended fatigue life by dissipating the stresses before they could build up and cause cracking. There were overstressed members in the shoulder and in other areas of the central pylon as well, but generally the frame was in sound condition.

The importance of the research and studies prepared during this phase was such that the American Society of Civil Engineers documented it for archival purposes.

There were other unequal stresses on the statue, unrelated to metal fatigue. They concerned the functioning of the statue's anchorage in the pedestal, which like a bridge anchorage keeps her from uplifting and overturning.

In the statue, all loads on the skin are transferred through the saddles to the armature bars and the springs and into the secondary

Dunnage beam, tie rods, and bolts.

Damaged lattice girders.

framework and the central pylon. From there, they are transferred down into the anchorage system embedded in the pedestal's massive concrete walls and finally into the foundation. The anchorage consists of two sets of massive cross beams, called dunnage beams, interconnected by giant vertical tension bars.

The upper set of dunnage beams takes downward loads, and the lower set resists the uplift resulting from lateral loads caused by wind forces. For optimal operation, the tension bars should be pretensioned to keep them from stretching out like rubber bands. This can be done by turning the bolt at the bottom of each bar. These bolts are 6 inches (15.2 centimeters) in diameter.

Thirty-ton hydraulic jacks were used to tighten the bolts to balance and tune the tension bars. These were not available to nineteenth-century workers. They used giant manual wrenches that have been preserved in the museum. Today, computerized instruments assisted in this task by measuring the exact tensile stresses obtained in each bar.

Investigating the statue's framework uncovered the fact that several of the five head-support arches were not properly attached to the

Acceleration gauges: Acceleration-gauge readings taken during the diagnostic stage indicated unequal stresses on the tension bars. There was no immediate danger except that the unevenly distributed stress reduced the framing system's overall safety factor. Under ordinary conditions, this would result in a small amount of uplift: the statue would lean and sway more than intended. However, under extreme wind conditions (the 100-year storm) there would be a greater danger of overturning or at least crushing the leeward side of the statue.

central pylon. These arches were reinforced and connected to the central pylon.

Lattice girders receive and frame the bottom folds of the draping copper robe, forming the outline for the pedestal cap. These girders were in poor condition. Sections had come in contact with the sagging robe and were almost completely corroded. Elsewhere portions of the top flange of the girders had been cut to allow the installation of guy rods, causing the girders to sag. These guy rods, installed at a very steep angle from the statue's framework, were intended to reduce the structure's tendency to topple. They never functioned as intended. The damaged portions of the girders were replaced and guy rods relocated to clear the lattice beams.

This completed the restoration of the metal framework. However, the general condition of the interior space needed improvement. Many coats of lead-based paint had to be removed from the iron framework and from the inner surface of the skin without damaging the copper.

There were many limitations. A flammable chemical solvent could not be used, as it might vaporize and explode in the unventilated interior. The statue, tall and narrow like a chimney flue, was vented only at the top, and the construction schedule required that the work be done during the summer, when temperatures inside could climb to more than 100°F (37.8°C). Also, the removed paint had to be contained as much as possible to prevent workers from inhaling lead.

For the inner surface of the skin, different chemicals or mechanical abrasives like walnut shells, glass beads, or ground corncob were considered. Methods utilizing heating or cooling were also investigated. A system using the freezing characteristics of liquid nitrogen was selected. Liquid nitrogen isn't flammable, will not explode, keeps the lead contained, and doesn't harm copper. On-site testing convinced everyone involved that this was the most appropriate method.

Masked workers sprayed the liquid nitrogen under pressure at a temperature of −320°F (−195.5°C). The frigid spray caused the paint to shrink and fall away from the surface of the copper like sheets of paper. It took ⅓ gallon (1.3 liters) of liquid nitrogen to remove 1 square foot (0.09 square meter) of paint. The interior surface covers 11,000 square feet (1022 square meters).

Liquid nitrogen removed the paint but did not remove a black layer of coal tar underneath the paint—the first layer that had been applied to the skin's interior, probably as waterproofing. It also didn't remove the paint from the armature bars. The armature grid showed up as never before against the black interior.

Only blasting would remove the coal tar. After comprehensive investigation of blasting agents, including rice and ground nut shells, the Park Service recommended using sodium bicarbonate. It is abrasive enough to remove the coal tar yet gentle enough not to harm the copper. Though the sodium bicarbonate worked well, it had the unfortunate side effect mentioned earlier of turning the patina blue. Also, because bicarbonate of soda easily absorbs moisture, it was necessary to install dehumidifiers (like hair dryers) to keep the blasting nozzles unclogged.

After the coal tar had been removed, the interior skin was washed with deionized water. This time, the skin turned from a natural-copper-penny color to green. Carbonates, trapped for years under the coal tar, were reacting with the water and the atmosphere. A "vinegar" wash with a carefully monitored pH level returned the copper to its natural color.

Paint still had to be removed from the central pylon and the secondary structure and the metal blasted to a "white metal" condition to eliminate the possibility of hidden corrosion. A vacuum device was added to the blasting equipment to avoid sending tons of grit billowing throughout the statue. A hand-held apparatus blasted sandy aluminum oxide along the surface of the iron. At the point of contact, a suction

Spraying liquid nitrogen.

Pedestal core and tunnel under renovation.

device immediately drew in the grit. This work was done day and night to complete it as quickly as possible.

The renovation of the tour of visitors through the pedestal and statue itself was our last task within the monument. The Port Authority of New York and New Jersey completed an exhaustive analysis of traffic flow in the pedestal and statue, which helped in our design. The new tour of the visit evolved only after the Park Service and the design team fully understood the limitations of the prerestoration systems.

Visitors now enter through the new monumental doors into the renovated two-story lobby containing the old torch and flame. Continuing straight toward the monument, they walk up a new grand stair. To either side, the stepped walls of the statue's foundation have been exposed so that visitors can see the very base of the monument.

The stone-and-concrete pedestal had a tall, hollow central core and four tunnel corridors on its axis at several levels. Its walls are as thick as many buildings are wide. The area between the fort wall and the pedestal's foundation is filled with earth. In the 1960s, a museum was added at the base of the pedestal. New exhibits that tell in wonderful detail the history of the statue construction and subsequent transformations have been installed in the museum levels.

Model of pedestal and stair system.

The strength of the pedestal and foundation concrete varies a great deal. But it is so massive that despite its crude qualities it had remained in good condition and needed little work.

The core was returned to its original 90-foot- (27.4-meter-) high space by removing the concrete floor slabs added at various times during the last 100 years. This allowed the installation of an appropriate stair system and a new glass-enclosed double-deck elevator that climbs within the cavernous interior.

The statue interior is an example of industrial structures in vogue at the end of the nineteenth century. The detailing is bold, and finishes are of the type encountered on a bridge or a battleship. We respected this in selecting materials and developing our detail vocabulary.

Through glass walls of the double-deck elevator, visitors can see the statue's massive anchorage system and the rough-hewn, board-formed concrete walls of the pedestal.

The lift travels slowly—about 200 feet (61 meters) per minute. Lighting on top and bottom of the elevator adds to the visitor's experience. A hydraulic-elevator system was used to avoid a bulky machine room at the balcony level. Rising 90 feet (27.4 meters), it is one of the tallest hydraulic-elevator systems in North America.

New pedestal stair.

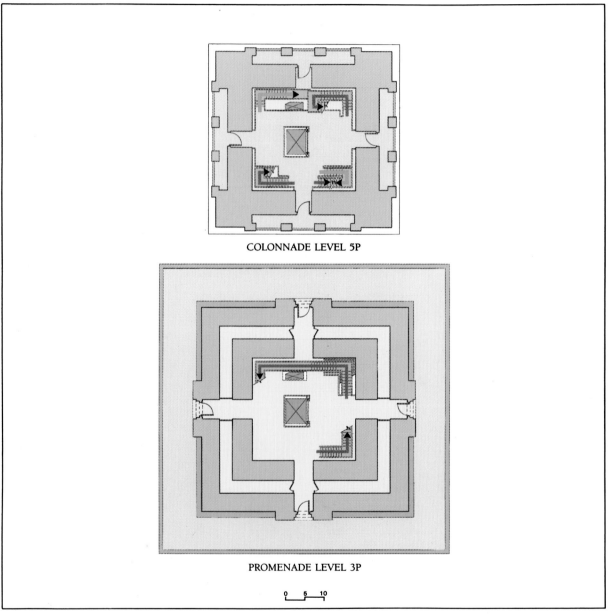

COLONNADE LEVEL 5P

PROMENADE LEVEL 3P

0   5   10

Plans of the pedestal at promenade and colon-
nade levels.

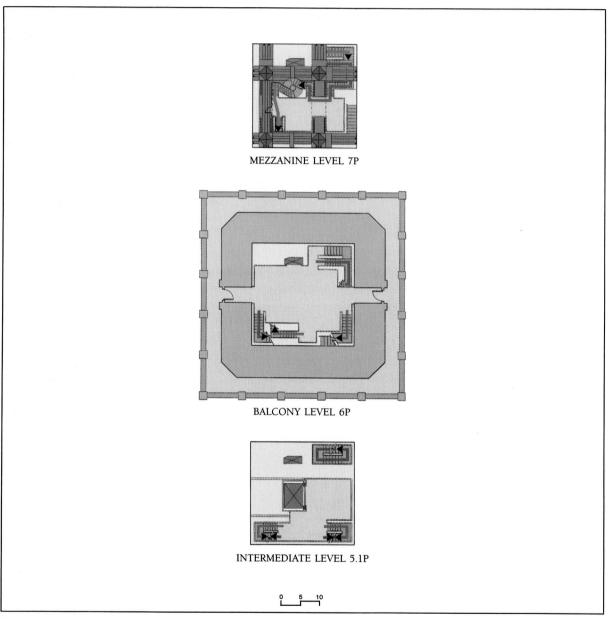

MEZZANINE LEVEL 7P

BALCONY LEVEL 6P

INTERMEDIATE LEVEL 5.1P

0   5   10

*Plans of pedestal at intermediate, balcony,
and mezzanine levels.*

Head platform.

Diagnostic report and tour of visit: The diagnostic report presented four proposals for the interior visit. The first called for moving visitors by retaining the existing elevator and helical stair, with minor improvements, and redesigning the crown observation platform to expand the viewing area and improve safety conditions. It also extended intermediate rest platforms outside the pylon for improved views of the interior.

The second called for the same redesign of the crown platform but changed the method of the climb dramatically. From the existing pedestal elevator, a new staircase was added outside the central tower. Stairs were wider and less steep than the helical stairs. This would have required removing structural members.

The third proposal called for a double-deck and glass-enclosed pedestal elevator with the new stairway outside the central tower.

The fourth proposal called for retaining the existing pedestal elevator and provided an inclinator from the balcony level to the lower portion of the shoulder. Below the shoulder, the spiral stair would be used for emergency egress, however. Two glass-enclosed cabs, each for ten people, were proposed for the inclinator. They moved very slowly to allow views of the interior and to keep vibrations to a minimum. This proposal required a drastic change to the secondary frame.

The adopted scheme incorporated features of each proposal while emphasizing and respecting the original structure.

The new elevator provides handicapped access. For the first time, physically challenged individuals can experience the interior of the monument and reach the colonnade level to enjoy harbor views.

The elevator unloads incoming visitors at the colonnade level and simultaneously loads departing visitors at a new intermediate level between the colonnade and the balcony. The balcony level was raised a few feet to align directly with the balcony outside, as it was originally.

Above the balcony level, the visitor suddenly discovers the beauty and mystery of the statue's interior: a magnificent space—a 110-foot- (33.5-meter-) high "room" of copper and metal, of light and shadow.

The restored double-spiral stair takes the visitor through this most unusual space. At five different levels during the climb, visitors can step off and walk around the helical stair to view the interior spaces.

The rest platforms allow the visitor to enjoy the full impact of the interior. They line up vertically as they extend outside the central pylon, like balconies on the side of a building, to minimize obstruction.

The 168-step spiral stair has been renovated by adding a new stainless-steel balustrade to replace the old battered one, cast stainless-steel steps to increase safety, and removing the rest seats that were originally provided every quarter turn. The seats interrupted the traffic flow as any person seated would block the path of everyone else behind.

The number of visitors making the climb will always be limited by the narrowness of the spiral stair and the size of the crown platform. Letters from tourists, young and old, telling of their ascent convinced us that the grueling climb was an integral part of the visitor's experience. Moreover, notwithstanding imaginative schemes for broader stair systems outside the central pylon, the helical stair is and remains the only practical way to gain access to the head platform without major modification to the statue's existing framework.

The steps to the head platform and the platform itself were modified to ease the flow of visitors. New windows were installed. The head platform is the statue's "lover's lane" and has always been a favorite spot. During the restoration when parties were given after hours to

A magnificent "room" of copper.

donors and sponsors, many romantic moments were recorded by the operating security cameras.

A small but crucial emergency elevator has been installed within the statue to give Park Service personnel prompt access from the base of the pedestal to the platform immediately below the statue's neck.

Before, if someone fell ill on the spiral stair, the rangers had to evacuate all the people behind that individual and then rush up the steps, bringing with them a folding stretcher similar to those used on ski slopes. The patient was put in the stretcher, which was hung on the outside of the stair balustrade, and then the trek down began, going around and around the spiral. If the patient was not seriously ill at the start of the descent, he or she certainly was upon reaching the base.

Using a laser surveying instrument, a way was found to fit the small, approximately 2- by 5-foot (0.6- by 1.5-meter) elevator cab without disturbing the existing structure. To avoid an obtrusive shaftway, a rack-and-pinion system, similar to those used in construction hoists and at the Eiffel Tower, was selected.

The heat, humidity, and excessive level of carbon dioxide inside the statue during the summer made visitors quite uncomfortable. The broad surface of the envelope heats like a copper kettle when exposed to the sun. If the statue were fully air-conditioned, a temperature and humidity differential would create a dew point and water would stream down the exterior or the interior as it does down an ice-filled drinking glass on a very warm day.

To avoid this, only mechanically circulating air ventilation has been provided. The humidity is squeezed out of the air by removing moisture as it passes through a refrigeration plant at the base of the statue.

A series of fans is installed in the pedestal and in the folds of the robe and vertical air-supply ducts located in the pylon legs, sized and shaped to be inconspicuous. The existing 16-inch- (40.6-centimeter-) diameter shaft of the spiral stair is used as a duct to deliver air to the head. The first test of the duct produced quite a large smoke puff in the head of the statue. All the dust accumulated in 100 years was suddenly blown away, and for a moment from outside the statue appeared to be smoking.

New interior lighting enhances the views. As with the exterior, the lighting allows a gradual revelation of spaces as one moves through the monument.

Throughout the renovation project our main goal was to expose, glorify, and enhance what existed: the drama of the spaces, the beauty of the structure, the excitement of the climb. If you leave the statue marveling at Hunt's boldness, Eiffel's ingenuity, and Bartholdi's vision, we have succeeded.

SYMBOL

Her heart is full, her door is still golden, her future bright. She has arms big enough to comfort and strong enough to support. For the strength in her arms is the strength of her people.

RONALD WILSON REAGAN
*President of the United States
from his address to the
Republican National Convention, 1984*

Dedicated to an ideal, not to the memory of battles or conquests, the statue has grown over the years to represent our most cherished values. She now symbolizes our nation, the land of liberty.

For the 17 million immigrants who passed her as they made their way through Ellis Island, she was and remains most special. The statue was their first vision at the end of a long and often grueling journey, and she held the promises of their dreams. This vision was passed to their children and their children's children. The statue's spirit has gone beyond the harbor.

The wonder of the statue is that while she represents America, she has become a universal symbol, transcending national boundaries, an image common to all people. Bartholdi used his mother's strong and stern facial features as the model for the statue. But the statue represents more than just a female image. The artist has imprinted the icon with a meaning that reaches deeply into the human unconscious: a comforting mother figure, demanding yet protective, a symbol of human aspiration. More than any other monument, the statue will remain as a testimony of our civilization for future generations.

The same dedication and hard work that guided all those who labored 100 years ago to build the statue and to give reality to their dream caught the nation again. From all corners, people volunteered their time or gave donations for the restoration of Liberty.

This great and generous nation as conceived by the founding fathers is as strong today as it has ever been. We are fortunate to witness a time when Americans are reveling in a renewed patriotic mood.

Throughout the project we were guided by a force that we couldn't see or touch. When the task at hand seemed almost impossible and the problems insurmountable, somehow the spirit of the statue always carried us along. Often enough at the end of a long day a child's query, "What did you do today?" and the answer, "I worked on the Statue of Liberty," were enough to renew our determination.

The land of liberty.

91

A team effort.

Once in a lifetime.

The statue's symbolism influenced many decisions. The helical staircase stays as part of the collective experience of millions. The upraised arm was repaired in place to avoid lowering it, even if temporarily. Whenever we climbed the scaffold, we felt her presence.

Our work would not have been complete without reflection. While reminiscing, we savored the friendships made and the camaraderie. The restoration was the epitome of a team effort. Very rarely does one feel like sharing the evening after spending a whole day working together on a project, but we often ended up around a dining table. We shared each other's cares and worries and bolstered each other's determination.

We will miss the morning boat rides, the late-night suppers, the good times and the bad. But we will remember. The flame alight in the harbor burns brightly within each of us. We see it in our dreams.

We did not have the usual feeling of creation on this project as when designing a building. We also did not have the usual feeling of loss at its end. The statue will always be ours because she belongs to everyone. And, hopefully, she always will.

Some structures are mute, some talk, some sing. We took one bursting with song and made it sing out even more. We have restored the statue's health without tampering with her dignity. And we are

grateful, proud, and privileged to have contributed to her immortality.

Her torch is raised; her scaffold is down. Our work is done; we have handed back the keys. As the doors open on her second century, the Statue of Liberty is as strong in body as in spirit.

She is alive and well, gracing New York harbor. She welcomes as never before all those who want to share in her dream.

95

*   *   *

"The New Colossus":
Not like the brazen giant of Greek fame,
With conquering limbs astride from land to
    land
Here at our sea-washed, sunset gates shall
    stand
A mighty woman with a torch, whose flame
Is the imprisoned lightning, and her name
Mother of Exiles. From her beacon-hand
Glows world-wide welcome, her mild eyes
    command
The air-bridged harbor that twin-cities
    frame.

"Keep, ancient lands, your storied pomp!"
    cries she
With silent lips. "Give me your tired, your
    poor,
Your huddled masses, yearning to breathe
    free,
The wretched refuse of your teeming shore.
Send these, the homeless, tempest tost, to
    me;
I lift my lamp beside the golden door!"
(Emma Lazarus, "The New Colossus,"
                    November 2, 1883.)

PERSPECTIVES

CHRONOLOGY

1834 Frédéric-Auguste Bartholdi is born in Colmar, France.

1855 Bartholdi establishes himself as a sculptor with a bronze statue of Gen. Jean Rapp.

1856 Bartholdi goes to Egypt to study ancient colossal works.

1865 Idea of a centennial gift to the United States to commemorate friendship during the American Revolution is born at a dinner party at Glatigny near Versailles held by the historian-politician Édouard de Laboulaye. Dinner guest Bartholdi embraces the idea.

1869 Bartholdi returns to Egypt for the dedication of the Suez Canal and unsuccessfully promotes a monumental lighthouse sculpture for the canal entrance.

1870 Franco-Prussian War delays the statue project, which had lain dormant during the politically unreceptive climate of Napoleon III's government.

1871 Bartholdi pays his first visit to the United States to propose the gift idea to influential Americans, including President Ulysses S. Grant, to choose a site, and to get to know the American people. The gift has taken shape as *La liberté éclairant le monde,* a colossal figure of a woman holding a torch for liberty.

1875 Bartholdi asks Eugène-Emmanuel Viollet-le-Duc to design the internal support system.

1875 The Third Republic comes to power in France. The political climate becomes more receptive to the statue. The French-American Union is formed, under the leadership of Laboulaye, to raise funds for the project. It includes twenty-two citizens, among them descendants of Rochambeau and Lafayette. Bartholdi exhibits the final model for the statue and work begins on the statue.

1876 The right hand, holding the torch and flame, is rushed to completion and previewed at the Centennial Exposition in Philadelphia to raise funds and interest in the project. After a year, it is moved to New York's Madison Square, where it remains for three years.

1877 Congress formally accepts the gift (prior to completion). A site is designated, and a committee to raise funds for a pedestal is formed.

1878 The statue's head is displayed at the Paris International Fair.

1879 Viollet-le-Duc dies at the age of sixty-four without having executed the design, except possibly for the head and torch and flame already completed. Eiffel becomes the designer of the internal support system.

1880 Bartholdi sketches the concept for the pedestal.

1881 U.S. Minister to France Levi P. Morton drives the first rivet hole (for the statue's left foot) for outdoor assembly in the Paris shop of Gaget, Gauthier & Cie.

1882 Richard Morris Hunt releases the first design for the pedestal.

1883 Laboulaye dies. Ferdinand de Lesseps, promotor of the Suez and Panama canals, replaces him as president of the French-American Union. Emma Lazarus publishes her poem "The New Colossus." Ground is broken for the statue's pedestal on Bedloe's Island.

1884 Assembly of the statue is completed in Paris. Morton formally accepts the gift.

1885 The statue is disassembled, crated, and shipped to the United States aboard the French state vessel *Isère*. It arrives in New York and is stored on the island to await completion of the pedestal. Joseph Pulitzer begins the pedestal fund-raising campaign. Americans in France promise Parisians a bronze replica of the statue, on a smaller scale, to be placed on the Seine's Ile des Cygnes.

1886 The pedestal completed, the statue is reassembled during the summer and unveiled on October 28. President Grover Cleveland and other notables attend the dedication ceremony. About 1 million people view the unveiling from boats and other vantage points in and around the harbor. Portholes are cut in the flame—without Bartholdi's approval—to make it a beacon.

1892 A belt of glass is added to the flame in an attempt to improve upon the disappointing porthole lighting scheme. Nearby Ellis Island opens as an immigration station.

1902 Statue is under the jurisdiction of the War Department as part of the Fort Wood army base.

1904 Bartholdi dies.

1905 Regilding is proposed for the flame at a cost $3500 but is never carried out.

1916 The flame, resculpted by Gutzon Borglum into a lantern of amber glass, is completed and dedicated by President Woodrow Wilson.

1924 The statue is declared a national monument. Massive waves of immigrants through Ellis Island cease.

1933 The statue is placed under jurisdiction of the National Park Service.

1936 Restoration for the fiftieth anniversary includes replacement of corroded armature bars, skin and spike repairs, and new lighting.

1954 Ellis Island closes as immigration station, having processed 17 million people in sixty-two years.

1956 Bedloe's Island is renamed Liberty Island.

1965 The Department of the Interior completes a stepped, two-story addition around the base of the pedestal for the Museum of Immigration.

1980 Aimé Millet's statue of Vercingetorix in France, which has a similar skin-attachment system, is restored.

1981 The French-American Committee forms. A white paper is presented to the National Park Service, revealing the statue's aged and weathered condition.

1982 Swanke Hayden Connell Architects and the Office of Thierry W. Despont become the French-American Committee's American architects for the restoration. President Ronald Reagan forms the Statue of

Liberty–Ellis Island Centennial Commission and names Lee A. Iacocca chairman. The Statue of Liberty–Ellis Island Foundation, Inc., is formed to raise funds from businesses and citizens to restore the statue and nearby Ellis Island for a combined $230 million. Public awareness and interest in the centennial restoration grow.

1983 A diagnostic report is presented to the Park Service.

1984 Swanke Hayden Connell Architects and The Office of Thierry W. Despont become architect and associate architect for the restoration on behalf of the Foundation. Study of the statue continues; the centennial restoration program is further developed and announced. Ammann & Whitney is selected as structural and mechanical consultant. Lehrer/McGovern is retained as construction manager. Construction work begins.

1984 The program for interior and pedestal renovation is announced, a scaffold is erected, the torch and flame are removed to be replaced, a workshed is built at the base, it is decided to repair rather than replace the shoulder framing, and interior paint is removed.

1985 A new armature is installed, and a new lobby is designed to display the old torch and flame. New monumental doors are designed, the new torch and flame are completed and installed, and the scaffold is removed.

1986 The work is complete. The statue's centennial is celebrated on July 3, 4, 5, and 6, and the statue is rededicated on October 28.

VITAL STATISTICS

The statue was surveyed in great detail during the restoration project. In some instances surveyed measurements were found to be at variance with Bartholdi's dimensions as given in his book *The Statue of Liberty Enlightening the World.* These discrepancies can be attributed to a variation in reference point (mean low-water mark, for example) or a difference in accuracy of measurement. When a difference was recorded, we give Bartholdi's dimensions first (B), then the surveyed dimensions (S).

Total height   305 feet 1 inch (93 meters) (B)
306 feet 8 inches (93.5 meters) (S)

Statue   151 feet 1 inch (46 meters) (B)
152 feet 2 inches (46.4 meters) (S)

Pedestal   154 feet (46.9 meters)

Statue

Heel to head   111 feet 1 inch (33.9 meters)

Right arm   42 feet (12.8 meters)

Right arm holding torch   45 feet (14 meters)

Greatest thickness of right arm   12 feet (3.7 meters)

Torch   21 feet (6.4 meters)

Head from neck to diadem   28 feet (8.5 meters)

Head thickness, ear to ear   10 feet (3 meters)

Eye width   2 feet 6 inches (0.76 meter)

Nose   3 feet 8 inches (1.1 meters)

Mouth width   3 feet (0.9 meter)

Length of hand   16 feet 5 inches (5 meters)

Nail width   1 foot 6 inches (0.46 meter)

Index-finger length   8 feet (2.4 meters)

Circumference of finger at second joint   4 feet 8 inches (1.4 meters)

Greatest thickness of waist   35 feet (10.7 meters)

Pre-1984 torch 250 panes of amber glass and nineteen lamps consuming 13,000 watts; lantern skylight of red and yellow glass

Head Twenty-five windows; accommodates twenty-five to thirty people at one time

Total weight 560,000 pounds (254,000 kilograms), 179,200 (81,300) of which is copper

Material 310 copper plates, about 3/32 inch (2.381 millimeters) thick, riveted together

Number of armature bars 1830

Number of saddles 2000 (approximate)

Number of armature rivets 12,000 (approximate)

Number of flat bars 325

Number of spiral steps 142

Number of new rest platforms 5

Height of emergency elevator 210 feet 2 inches (64 meters)

Pedestal

   Height of cavernous space 126 feet 7 inches (38.6 meters)

   Height of new elevator 95 feet 2 inches (29 meters)

   Number of dunnage beams Four in each of two sets

   Number of anchor bars Sixteen in groups of four

   Height of stairway 126 feet 7 inches (38.6 meters)

ORGANIZATIONS

The project was funded and administered by the Statue of Liberty–Ellis Island Foundation (the client) on behalf of the United States government, represented by the National Park Service of the Department of the Interior (the owner). The design team was led by Swanke Hayden Connell as architect and The Office of Thierry W. Despont as associate architect. Lehrer/McGovern was the firm responsible for the construction management of the project and the coordination of the trade contractors.

Client

The Statue of Liberty–Ellis Island Foundation
101 Park Avenue
New York, New York   10178

Owner

National Park Service of the Department of the Interior
18th and C Streets, N.W.
Washington, D.C.   20240

Architects and Engineers

Swanke Hayden Connell   *Architect*
400 Park Avenue
New York, New York   10022

The Office of Thierry W. Despont   *Associate architect*
335 Greenwich Street
New York, New York   10013

Ammann & Whitney, Inc.   *Structural and mechanical*
2 World Trade Center   *engineer*
New York, New York   10048

Howard Brandston Lighting Design, Inc. 141 West 24th Street New York, New York 10011	*Lighting consultants*
John A. Van Deusen and Associates, Inc. 100 West Mount Pleasant Avenue Livingston, New Jersey 07039	*Elevator consultants*
W. A. DiGiacomo Associates 1250 Broadway New York, New York 10001	*Mechanical and electrical engineers for the museum*

French Groupement of Consultants

Care of Constructa
13 Rue Gandon
75013 Paris
France

Construction Manager and Contractors

Lehrer/McGovern, Inc. 387 Park Avenue South New York, New York 10016	*Construction manager*
Alimak Incorporated 1100 Boston Avenue Bridgeport, Connecticut 06608	*Emergency elevators*
Ben Strauss Industries 36–03 Greenpoint Avenue Long Island City, New York 11101	*Coatings removal*
Grossman Steel & Aluminum Corp. 375 Western Highway Tappan, New York 10983	*Stairs*
Kerby-Saunders, Inc. 575 8th Avenue New York, New York 10018	*Heating, ventilating, and air conditioning*
Les Métalliers Champenois Represented by Kevin MacCarthy Associates 485 Madison Avenue New York, New York 10022	*Torch and flame*
2a Rue des Létis 51500 Benzannes-les-Reims France	
NAB Construction 112–20 14th Avenue College Point, New York 11356	*Ornamental and structural steel*
NAB/Fiebiger—A Joint Venture 112–20 14th Avenue College Point, New York 11356	*Armatures and skin repairs*
National Elevator 63–69 East 24th Street Paterson, New Jersey 07514	*Elevators*
Pace Plumbing Corp. 41 Box Street Brooklyn, New York 11222	*Plumbing*
Tacro P.O. Box 805 Warrendale, Pennsylvania 15095	*Windows*

101

Universal Builders Supply, Inc. 216 South Terrace Avenue Mount Vernon, New York 10550	*Rigging and scaffolding*
Urban Foundation, Inc. 32–33 111th Street P.O. Box 158 East Elmhurst, New York 11369	*Structural concrete*
Wade Electrical Contracting Co. 84–48 129th Street Kew Gardens, New York 11415	*Electrical work*
P. A. Fiebiger 462 Tenth Avenue New York, New York 10018	*Armatures and skin repairs*

GLOSSARY

anchorage Double set of massive cross beams interconnected by vertical tension bars and embedded in the massive concrete of the pedestal to keep the statue from overturning.

anemometer Instrument that measures the speed of the wind.

anneal To free from internal stress by sudden heating and cooling.

armature Statue's network of iron straps that conform to the folds of the copper envelope and give it support.

asbestos isolator Material provided by Alexandre-Gustave Eiffel to separate and prevent electrolytic reaction between the copper skin and the iron armature that supports it.

balcony Balustraded platform that projects from the pedestal on all four sides and provides the public with the highest access on the exterior. It was used as an entry for workers during restoration work.

balustrade Railing with closely spaced vertical supports.

carbonates Salts and esters of carbonic acid (carbon dioxide dissolved in water) formed when exposed to sodium bicarbonate and the saline environment around the statue that temporarily turned the exterior blue and the interior green during cleaning.

Charpy impact test Test that measures stress propagation—the spread of cracks—in metals used in determining the condition of the statue's puddled-iron framework.

central pylon Primary framing system and backbone of the statue—a central iron tower consisting of four legs connected by cross bracing and bolted at their lower ends to the anchorage.

colonnade Two-story-high columned opening in the pedestal on each face directly below the balcony that, inside, is the upper terminus for the lower (unloading) cab of the new double-decked elevator.

compagnon Master craftsperson (literally, mate, fellow).

contrapposto Stance with one foot forward common in classical sculpture that makes a figure appear stationary from the front and moving forward from the side.

deionized water Water used to rinse or clean the statue that is ion-free (chargeless) to avoid oxidation that would affect the patina.

diadem Crown.

diaphragm Solid plate inserted at the head and shoulder to reinforce the statue's framework.

Doric Designating one of five classic Greek orders: an arrangement of columns with an entablature.

Doric socle The forty shields on the pedestal that were meant to carry the coats of arms of the states.

double-helix stair Double-spiral stairway that rises within the central pylon to allow visitors to climb to the crown by providing separate up and down systems.

dunnage beams Giant cross beams embedded in the walls of the pedestal that are the main elements in the statue's anchorage.

electrolytic reaction Chemical reaction caused by the passage of electric current between two dissimilar metals (in this case, iron and copper) in contact with themselves and moisture. The reaction results in the corrosion, swelling, and eventual disintegration of the less noble of the two metals.

electroplating Coating or plating a metal by electrolysis, through either dipping or brushing on.

ferallium High-strength, low-corrosion steel alloy (used by the British Navy as a bronze replacement) employed for the flat-bar spring replacements in the statue's framework.

foundation The 64-foot- (19.5-meter-) tall tapering concrete base of the statue's tall pedestal that provides the mass needed to keep the statue upright.

gilding Coating with gold, gold leaf, or a gold-colored substance. The statue's original flame was gilded copper.

gold leaf Thin layer of gold applied over an object and the application chosen to gild the restored flame.

golden ratio System of proportions used as a guiding principal in classical architecture to ensure elegance and beauty. The relationship of the axis of the statue's central pylon to the square interior shaft of the pedestal reflects the application of this principle by Richard Morris Hunt.

gueule de loup Precise metal joinery without rivets or screws that resembles the closed teeth of a wolf, used on the statue to connect copper plates of the nose on the statue (literally, wolf's mouth).

guy bars The eight stabilizing bars extending at an angle from the primary framework through the lattice girders to the cross beams that were installed too steeply to function as efficiently as intended.

hydraulic elevator Elevator that relies on fluid pressure for locomotion and needs no machine room overhead.

inclinator Elevator that travels on an incline.

lattice girder Girder with top and bottom flanges connected by latticework—metal cross strips on the diagonal. Lattice girders outline the cap of the statue's pedestal as well as the base of the robe.

liquid nitrogen Liquid form of the common gas often used in cooling that was employed to remove seven layers of paint from the inner surface of the statue's copper envelope by freezing and thereby shrinking off the paint.

metal fatigue Weakening, breakdown, or failure of metal subjected to continued stress or cycles of stress. Fatigue life: the number of applications of a given stress applied to a metal sample before it fails.

metal halide lamp Compound light filament that is extremely efficient.

mezzanine New inside level in the pedestal between the colonnade and the balcony that is the landing for the upper (and loading) cab of the double-decked elevator.

passivation Treating a metal to render its surface less reactive chemically. At the statue it was used to bring back the chromium protective finish to the surface of the stainless-steel armature bars.

patina Sometimes protective film or encrustation, usually green, produced by oxidation on the surface of old bronze or copper.

pedestal The 90-foot- (27.4-meter-) tall rusticated-granite-covered massive concrete structure designed by Richard Morris Hunt on which the statue stands. It has concrete walls as thick as 20 feet (6.1 meters) and contains the statue's giant anchorage.

pendant Bottom tip of the torch handle, in the shape of an acorn, that had become the repository of an unwelcome mixture including water, bird droppings, and rust.

Pharos I and II Richard Morris Hunt's study models for the statue pedestal.

preservation In architecture, maintaining a structure as it is, including changes and additions, to provide a visual historic record of its life.

primary framework Central pylon or tower of the statue's skeleton that is the backbone of its support system.

puddled iron French relative of wrought iron known for its impurities.

repoussé Hammering on the reverse side of a metal to give it shape, form, or relief.

restoration "To restore an edifice. It is not to maintain, repair or rebuild it, it is to reestablish it in complete state which may never have existed at any given time." (Viollet-le-Duc, *Dictionary,* 1845–1868.)

"Restoration . . . stops where hypothesis begins: beyond that any additional work needed is part of architectural creation and will bear the mark of its time." (Article 9 of the Charter of Venice, 1964.)

Differences in attitudes toward restoration have never been resolved (probably never will be) and are subject to the sociological outlook as well as the technological capabilities of the time.

saddles Brackets that wrap around the armature bars and are riveted to the copper skin to attach the skin to the armature indirectly.

scaffold Temporary structure for holding workers or materials during the erection, repair, or decoration of a building or permanent structure.

sculpture Art of carving, modeling, welding, or otherwise producing figurative or abstract works of art in three dimensions.

secondary framework System of triangulated support bars between the primary framework and the armature in a rough outline of the statue's figure.

sodium bicarbonate Mild abrasive powder used to remove the coal tar that had been applied to the inner surface of the copper skin.

stainless steel 316L Low-strength, low-carbon stainless steel that is typically used for equipment in the food service industry but is used on the statue to replace its iron armature.

strain gauge Instrument applied to an object to measure stress imposed by wind and other forces.

structure Something built or constructed, as a building, bridge, dam, etc.; mode of building, construction, or organization; arrangement of parts, elements, or constituents; complex system considered from the point of view of the whole.

symbol Something used or regarded as representing something else; material object representing something, often something immaterial.

Teflon tape Polytetrafluoroethylene mastic used in the statue to separate the surfaces of copper and stainless steel in the armature to prevent electrolytic reaction.

tension bars Vertical flat iron bars, 62 feet (18.9 meters) long, that extend from and connect the upper set of cross beams to the lower set, in groups of four each at the ends of the beams. The sixteen anchor bars are bolted under the lower set of beams, and the bolts can be tuned so that there is equal stress on each bar and minimal uplift in the statue.

ultrasonic caliper Instrument attached to a surface of a material that uses nonaudible frequencies to measure its thickness without harming it in any way.

xenon Chemically inactive gas used for luminescent tubes.

DRAWINGS

I n the course of the project more than 200 architectural and engineering drawings were prepared to document in minute detail the statue's condition and the work of the centennial restoration. The following plates were prepared from those drawings to illustrate the complexity and uniqueness of the monument.

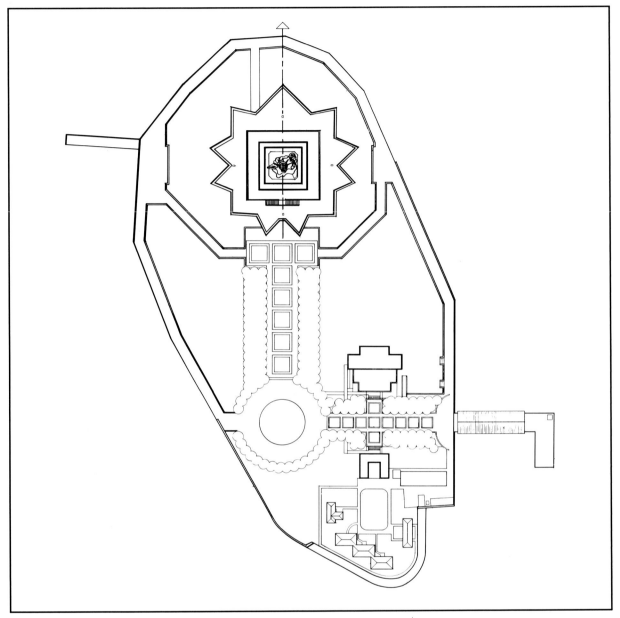

**CENTENNIAL RESTORATION OF
THE STATUE OF LIBERTY**

II
The Monument

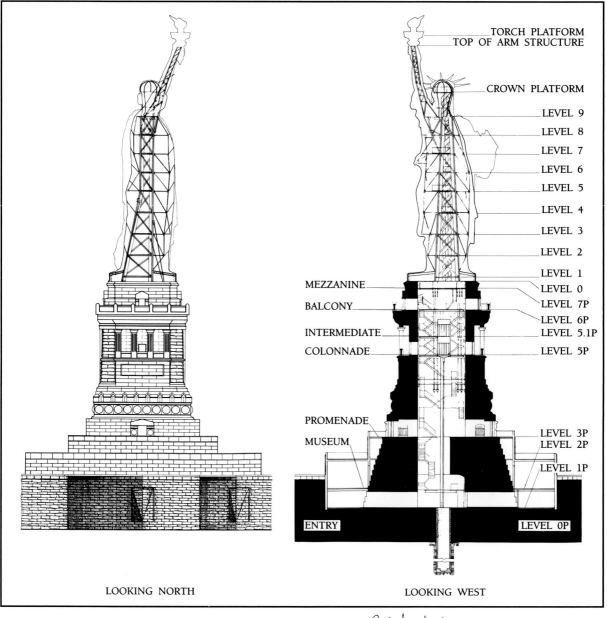

TORCH PLATFORM
TOP OF ARM STRUCTURE

CROWN PLATFORM

LEVEL 9
LEVEL 8
LEVEL 7
LEVEL 6
LEVEL 5
LEVEL 4
LEVEL 3
LEVEL 2
LEVEL 1

MEZZANINE — LEVEL 0
BALCONY — LEVEL 7P
— LEVEL 6P
INTERMEDIATE — LEVEL 5.1P
COLONNADE — LEVEL 5P

PROMENADE
MUSEUM
LEVEL 3P
LEVEL 2P
LEVEL 1P

ENTRY   LEVEL 0P

LOOKING NORTH   LOOKING WEST

CENTENNIAL RESTORATION OF
THE STATUE OF LIBERTY

III
Statue Structure
(computer diagram)

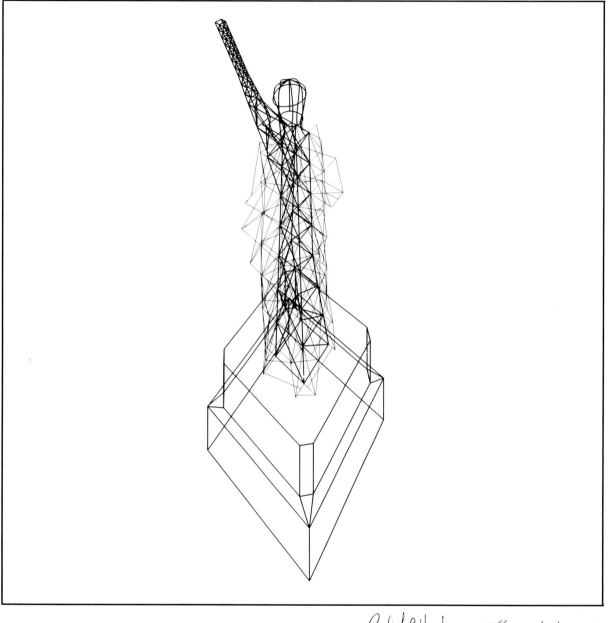

CENTENNIAL RESTORATION OF
THE STATUE OF LIBERTY

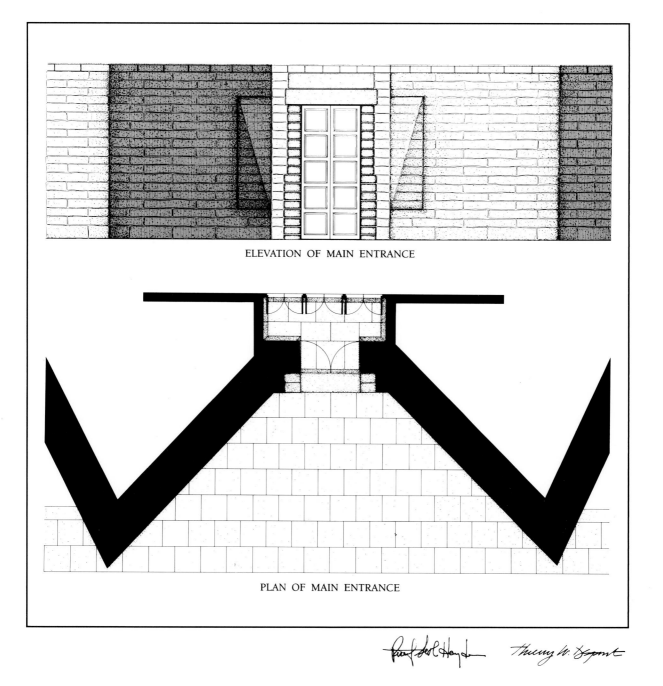

ELEVATION OF MAIN ENTRANCE

PLAN OF MAIN ENTRANCE

CENTENNIAL RESTORATION OF
THE STATUE OF LIBERTY

V
Entrance Hall

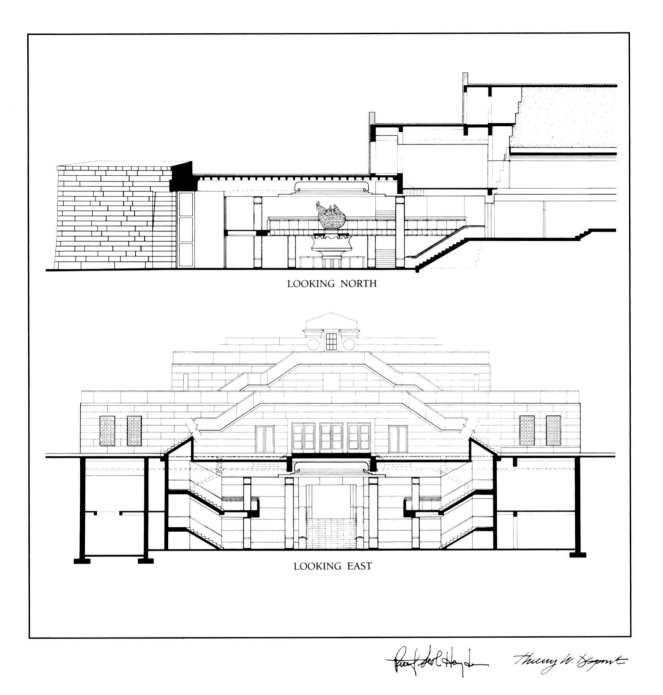

LOOKING NORTH

LOOKING EAST

CENTENNIAL RESTORATION OF
THE STATUE OF LIBERTY

VI
Plan of Pedestal

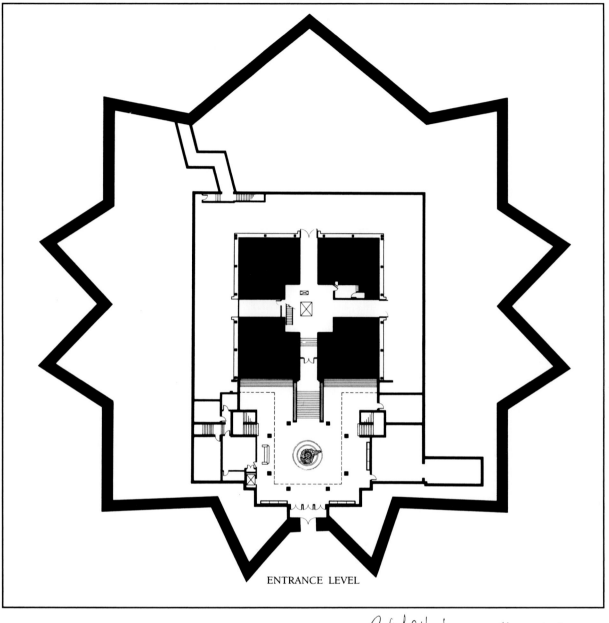

ENTRANCE LEVEL

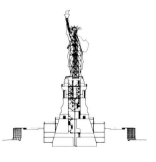

**CENTENNIAL RESTORATION OF
THE STATUE OF LIBERTY**

Plans of Pedestal

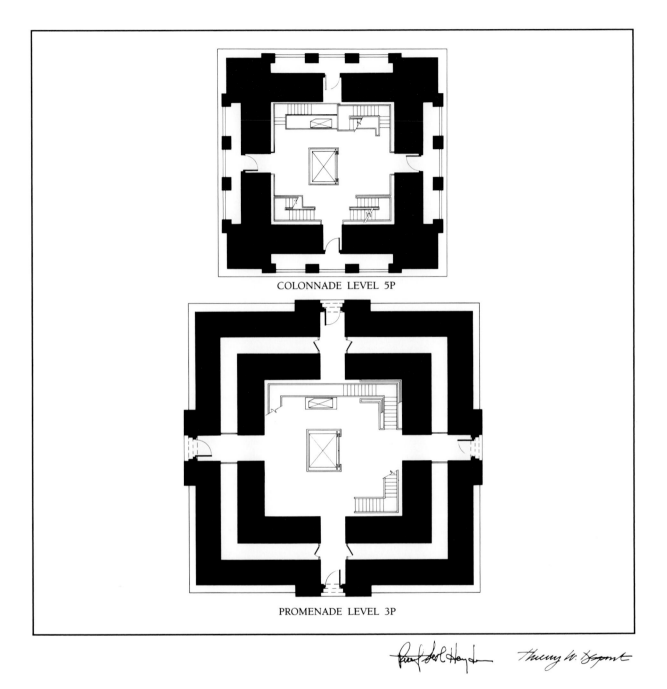

COLONNADE LEVEL 5P

PROMENADE LEVEL 3P

CENTENNIAL RESTORATION OF
THE STATUE OF LIBERTY

VIII
Plans of Pedestal

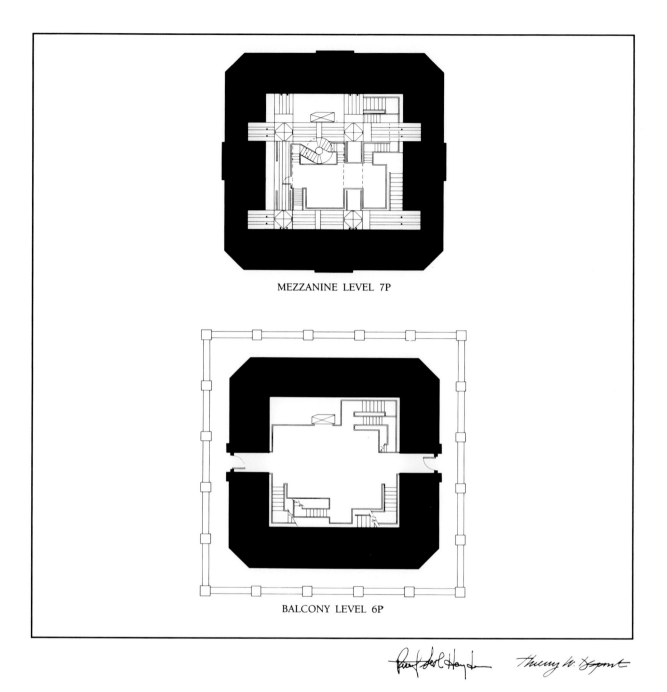

MEZZANINE LEVEL 7P

BALCONY LEVEL 6P

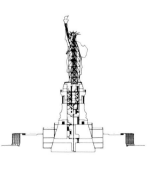

CENTENNIAL RESTORATION OF
THE STATUE OF LIBERTY

IX
Section of Pedestal

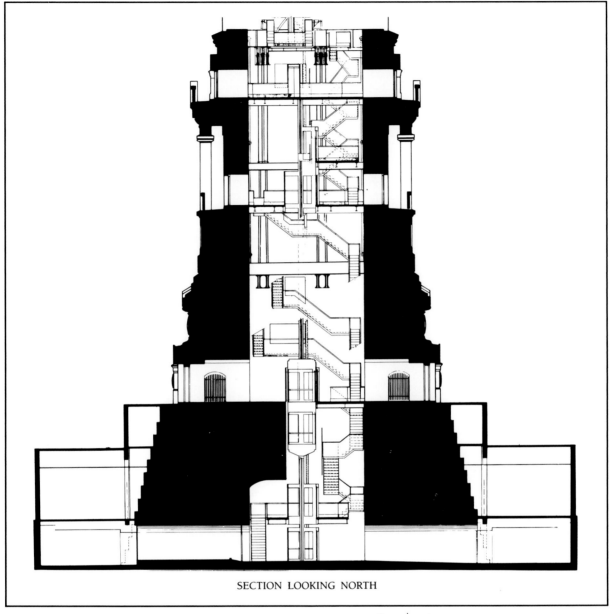

SECTION LOOKING NORTH

CENTENNIAL RESTORATION OF
THE STATUE OF LIBERTY

X
Plans of Statue

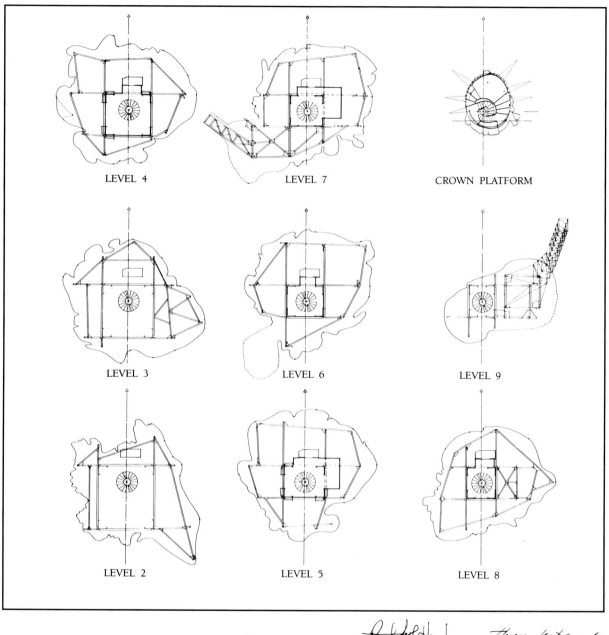

LEVEL 4   LEVEL 7   CROWN PLATFORM

LEVEL 3   LEVEL 6   LEVEL 9

LEVEL 2   LEVEL 5   LEVEL 8

**CENTENNIAL RESTORATION OF
THE STATUE OF LIBERTY**

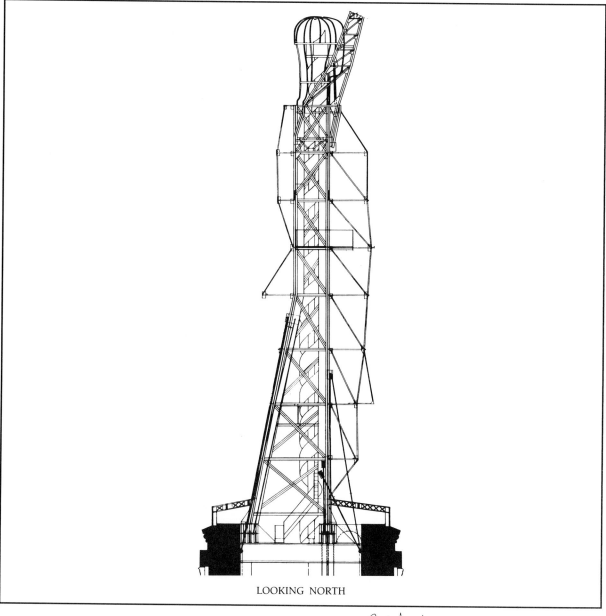

LOOKING NORTH

**CENTENNIAL RESTORATION OF
THE STATUE OF LIBERTY**

XII
Shoulder Structure

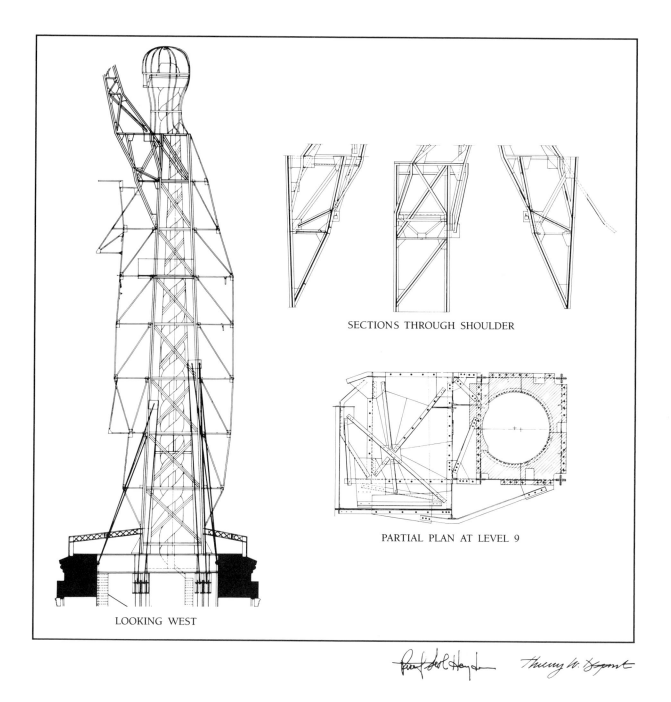

SECTIONS THROUGH SHOULDER

PARTIAL PLAN AT LEVEL 9

LOOKING WEST

XIII
Armature

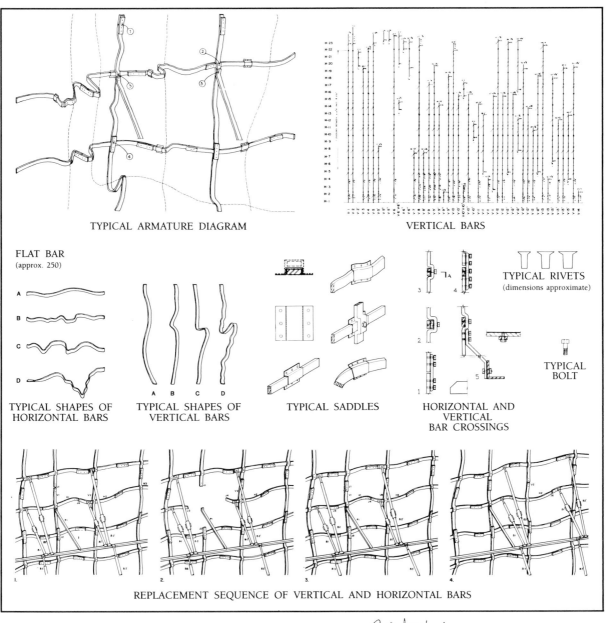

TYPICAL ARMATURE DIAGRAM

VERTICAL BARS

FLAT BAR
(approx. 250)

A

B

C

D

TYPICAL SHAPES OF
HORIZONTAL BARS

A B C D

TYPICAL SHAPES OF
VERTICAL BARS

TYPICAL SADDLES

TYPICAL RIVETS
(dimensions approximate)

TYPICAL
BOLT

HORIZONTAL AND
VERTICAL
BAR CROSSINGS

1. 2. 3. 4.

REPLACEMENT SEQUENCE OF VERTICAL AND HORIZONTAL BARS

CENTENNIAL RESTORATION OF
THE STATUE OF LIBERTY

XIV
Helical Stair

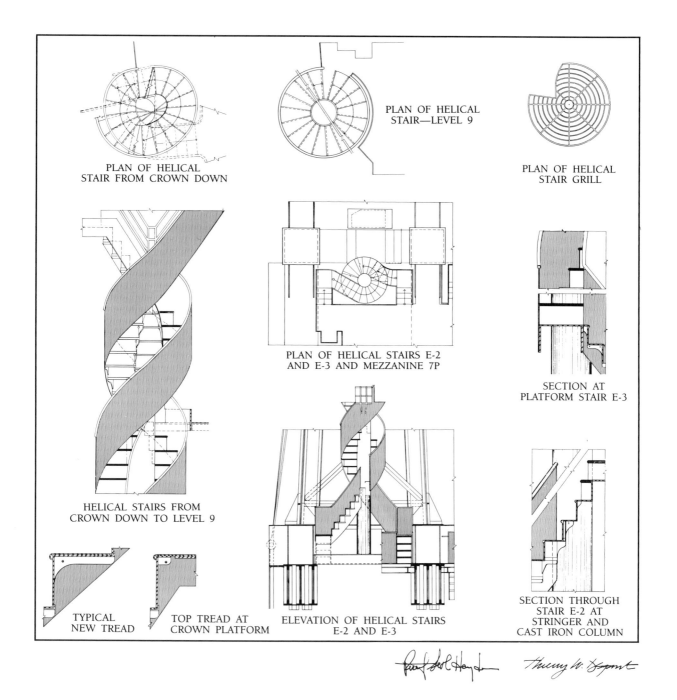

PLAN OF HELICAL
STAIR FROM CROWN DOWN

PLAN OF HELICAL
STAIR—LEVEL 9

PLAN OF HELICAL
STAIR GRILL

HELICAL STAIRS FROM
CROWN DOWN TO LEVEL 9

PLAN OF HELICAL STAIRS E-2
AND E-3 AND MEZZANINE 7P

SECTION AT
PLATFORM STAIR E-3

TYPICAL
NEW TREAD

TOP TREAD AT
CROWN PLATFORM

ELEVATION OF HELICAL STAIRS
E-2 AND E-3

SECTION THROUGH
STAIR E-2 AT
STRINGER AND
CAST IRON COLUMN

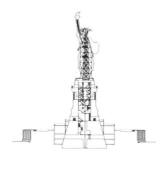

CENTENNIAL RESTORATION OF
THE STATUE OF LIBERTY

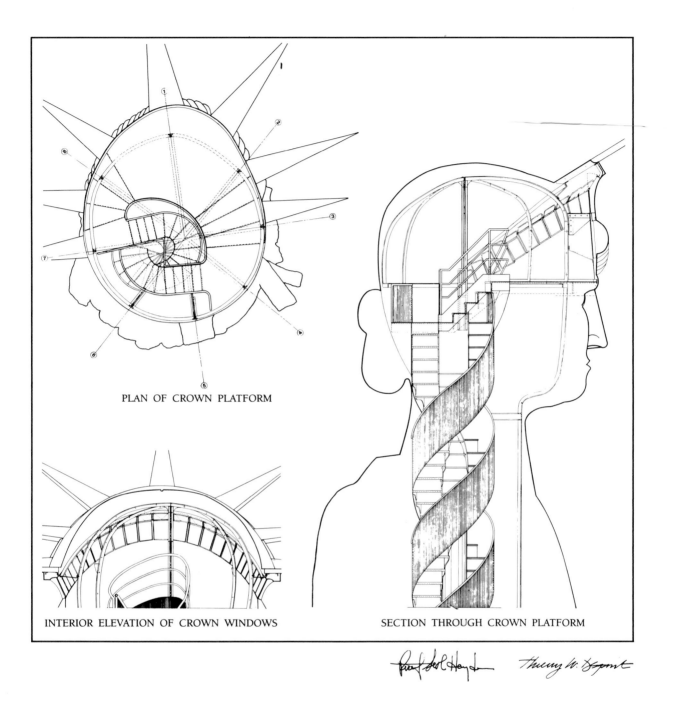

PLAN OF CROWN PLATFORM

INTERIOR ELEVATION OF CROWN WINDOWS

SECTION THROUGH CROWN PLATFORM

CENTENNIAL RESTORATION OF
THE STATUE OF LIBERTY

XVI
Torch and Flame

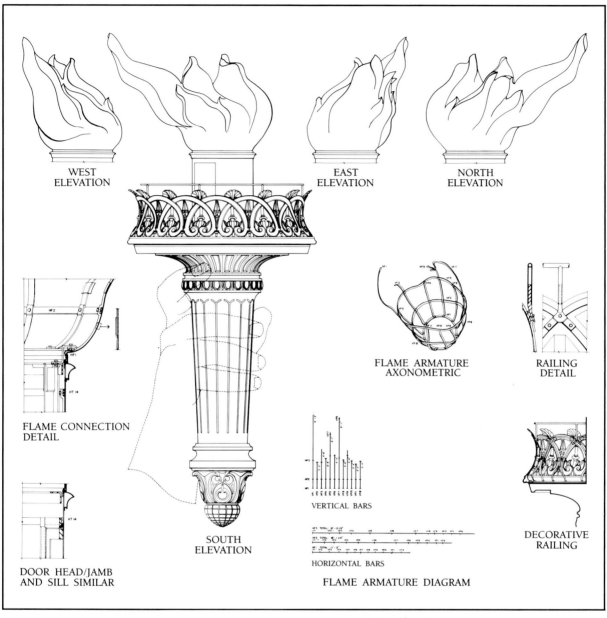

WEST
ELEVATION

EAST
ELEVATION

NORTH
ELEVATION

FLAME ARMATURE
AXONOMETRIC

RAILING
DETAIL

FLAME CONNECTION
DETAIL

VERTICAL BARS

HORIZONTAL BARS

SOUTH
ELEVATION

FLAME ARMATURE DIAGRAM

DECORATIVE
RAILING

DOOR HEAD/JAMB
AND SILL SIMILAR

CENTENNIAL RESTORATION OF
THE STATUE OF LIBERTY

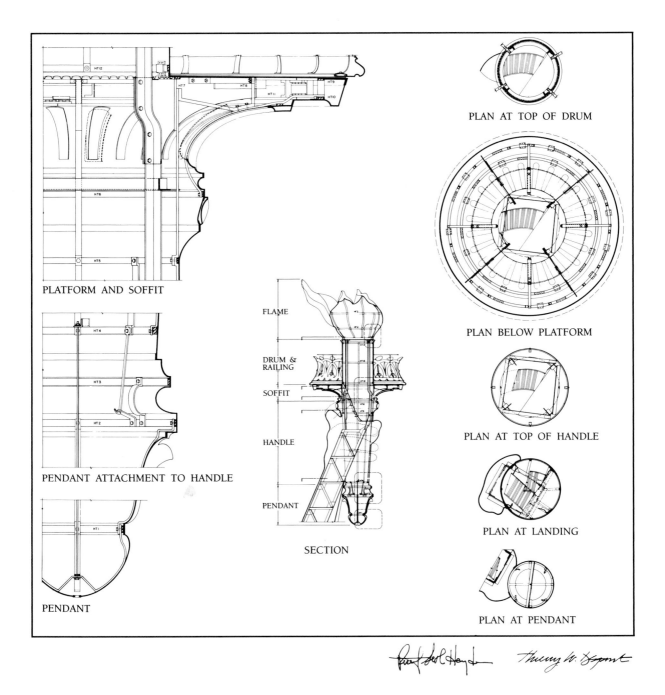

PLATFORM AND SOFFIT

PENDANT ATTACHMENT TO HANDLE

PENDANT

FLAME

DRUM & RAILING

SOFFIT

HANDLE

PENDANT

SECTION

PLAN AT TOP OF DRUM

PLAN BELOW PLATFORM

PLAN AT TOP OF HANDLE

PLAN AT LANDING

PLAN AT PENDANT

**CENTENNIAL RESTORATION OF
THE STATUE OF LIBERTY**

XVIII
Old Flame
(computer photogrammetry)

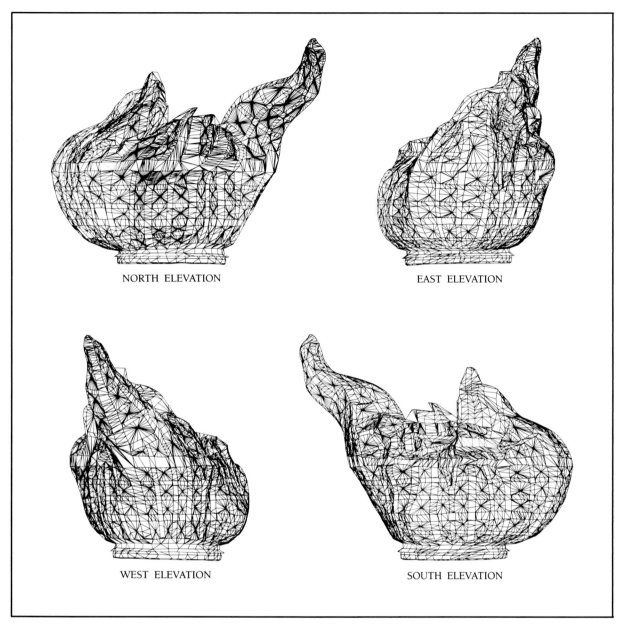

NORTH ELEVATION

EAST ELEVATION

WEST ELEVATION

SOUTH ELEVATION

CENTENNIAL RESTORATION OF
THE STATUE OF LIBERTY

XIX
New Flame
(computer photogrammetry)

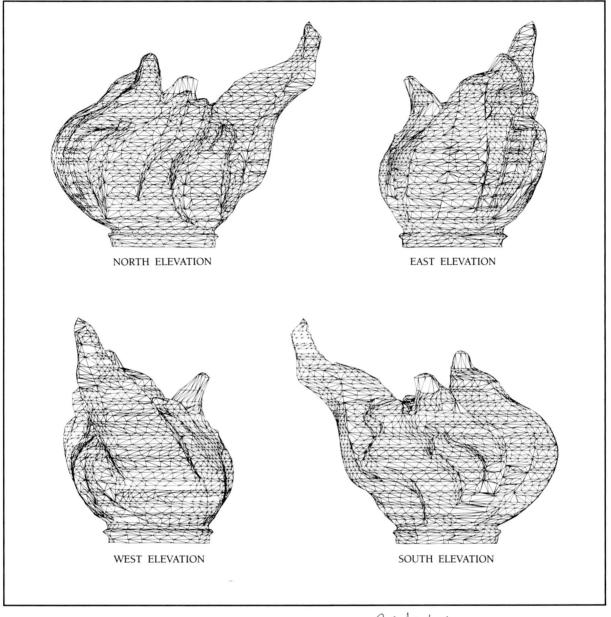

NORTH ELEVATION

EAST ELEVATION

WEST ELEVATION

SOUTH ELEVATION

**CENTENNIAL RESTORATION OF
THE STATUE OF LIBERTY**

XX

Views of Statue

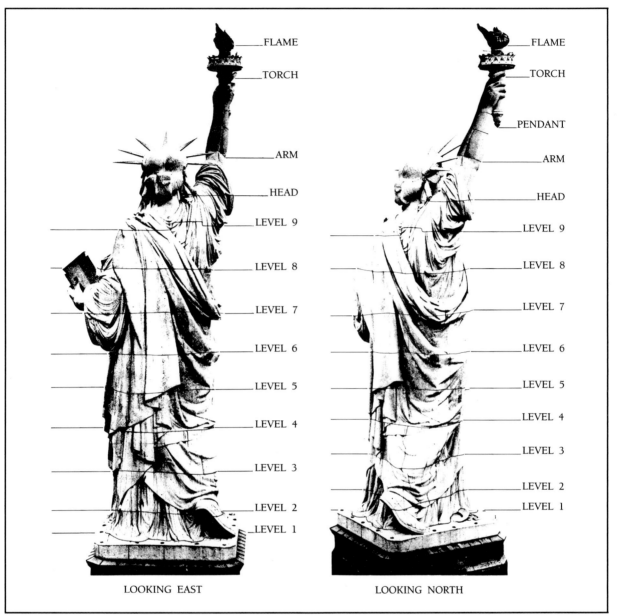

FLAME

TORCH

ARM

HEAD

LEVEL 9

LEVEL 8

LEVEL 7

LEVEL 6

LEVEL 5

LEVEL 4

LEVEL 3

LEVEL 2

LEVEL 1

LOOKING EAST

FLAME

TORCH

PENDANT

ARM

HEAD

LEVEL 9

LEVEL 8

LEVEL 7

LEVEL 6

LEVEL 5

LEVEL 4

LEVEL 3

LEVEL 2

LEVEL 1

LOOKING NORTH

**CENTENNIAL RESTORATION OF
THE STATUE OF LIBERTY**

XXI
Views of Statue

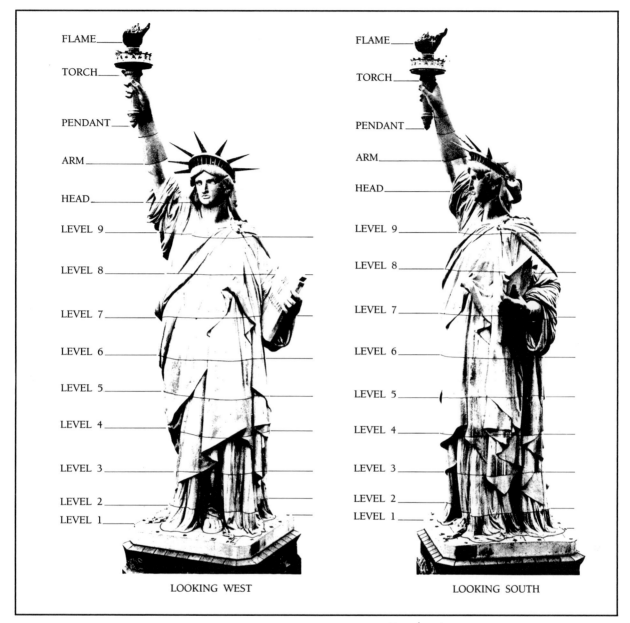

FLAME

TORCH

PENDANT

ARM

HEAD

LEVEL 9

LEVEL 8

LEVEL 7

LEVEL 6

LEVEL 5

LEVEL 4

LEVEL 3

LEVEL 2

LEVEL 1

LOOKING WEST

FLAME

TORCH

PENDANT

ARM

HEAD

LEVEL 9

LEVEL 8

LEVEL 7

LEVEL 6

LEVEL 5

LEVEL 4

LEVEL 3

LEVEL 2

LEVEL 1

LOOKING SOUTH

CENTENNIAL RESTORATION OF
THE STATUE OF LIBERTY

BIBLIOGRAPHY

Baker, Paul R.: *Richard Morris Hunt,* M.I.T., Cambridge, Mass., and London, 1980.

Bartholdi, Frédéric-Auguste: "The Statue of Liberty Enlightening the World," *North American Review,* New York, 1885.

"Bartholdi," *Annuaire de la Société d'Histoire et d'Archéologie de Colmar,* 1979.

Bell, James B., and Richard I. Abrams: *In Search of Liberty,* Doubleday, Garden City, N.Y., 1984.

Blanchet, Christian, and Bertrand Dard: *Statue de la Liberté,* Edition Comet's Distribution Vilo, Paris, 1984.

George, Michael: *The Statue of Liberty,* Abrams, New York, 1985.

Gustave Eiffel et son temps, Galerie du Messager, Paris, 1983.

Handlin, Oscar, and the Editors of the Newsweek Book Division: *Statue of Liberty,* Newsweek Book Division, New York, 1971.

Lemoine, Bertrand: *Gustave Eiffel,* Jean Mussot, Paris, 1980.

Marrey, Bertrand: *La vie et l'oeuvre extraordinaires de Monsieur Gustave Eiffel,* Graphite, Paris, 1984.

Mercer, Charles E.: *Statue of Liberty,* Putnam, New York, 1979.

Nash, Margo: *Statue of Liberty,* Manhattan Post Card Publishing, Glendale, N.Y., 1983.

Schmitt, Jean-Marie: *Cent ans d'études bartholdiennes,* Archives Municipales de Colmar, Colmar, 1985.

Trachtenberg, Marvin: *The Statue of Liberty,* Penguin, London, 1976.

Viollet-le-Duc, Galerie Nationale du Grand Palais, Paris, 1980

INDEX

Page numbers in *italic* indicate illustrations or sidebars.

151